A Note to Readers

The Allerton and Fisk families are fictional, but the events they find themselves in actually happened. During 1893, the United States celebrated the four hundredth anniversary of Columbus arriving in America. A huge world's fair in Chicago was dedicated in 1892 and opened to visitors in 1893. One of the major attractions was the first Ferris wheel, which towered over everything else on the grounds.

But many people weren't in the mood for a party. One of the worst financial disasters to ever hit the United States threw hundreds of thousands of people out of work. Banks closed. Railroads went out of business. People faced starvation. And in Minneapolis, a major fire destroyed businesses and homes.

The idea that Esther and Ted think of to help so many poor families actually was thought of by children in Minneapolis at the time. They played a large role in making adults aware of how big the problem of hunger in their city was.

CHICAGO
WORLD'S FAIR

JoAnn A. Grote

BARBOUR
PUBLISHING, INC.
Uhrichsville, Ohio

To Donna Winters, friend and fellow writer. Thank you for your assistance in researching The Columbian Exposition.

Published by Barbour Publishing, Inc.
P.O. Box 719
Uhrichsville, Ohio 44683
http://www.barbourbooks.com

ecpa Member of the
Evangelical Christian
Publishers Association

Printed in the United States of America.

Cover illustration by Peter Pagano.
Inside illustrations by Adam Wallenta.

CHAPTER 1

Danger at the Bank

Twelve-year-old Esther Allerton leaned close to her cousin Ted Fisk, who shared the double wooden school desk. "What do you think the teachers keep meeting about?" she whispered in his ear.

Ted's almost-black eyes turned toward tall, lanky Mr. Evans and short, stout Mr. Timms where they stood in the doorway. Mr. Evans shoved his round, wire-rimmed glasses up his skinny nose, all the time whispering furiously to Mr. Timms. Mr. Timms pressed his lips tightly together and shook his head, his round cheeks bouncing.

"I don't know," Ted whispered back. "This is the third time Mr. Evans has come to our room this morning."

One of Mr. Evans's long arms shot out, and he pounded a fist in the air between himself and Mr. Timms. His pointed chin stuck out defiantly. Esther couldn't hear everything he said, but one phrase reached her ears.

She whipped her head toward Ted. He stared back at her, his eyes as wide as she knew her own must be.

"Did he say 'Farmers' and Mechanics' Bank'?" she asked.

Ted nodded. "That's where Uncle Enoch works."

"Why would Mr. Evans be upset about the bank?"

"I heard Father and Mother talking after church yesterday about the bank. They said there was a rumor in the city that the bank doesn't have enough money."

"How can a bank not have enough money? Doesn't money come from banks?"

Ted shrugged, his shoulders lifting the brown jacket that covered his white shirt with its round collar. "I don't know, but the rumor said the bank was going to close."

Fear tightened Esther's stomach. "Would Uncle Enoch lose his job?"

Ted rolled his eyes. "Uncle Enoch isn't going to lose his job. It's just a rumor. Father says the bank is solid as rock."

"Whew." Esther's stomach felt normal again. She'd heard her parents talk about hard times in the country. Money was tight and people were losing their jobs. She didn't want Uncle Enoch to be one of those people.

The lunch bell rang, cutting off her thoughts. Mr. Evans dashed away. The students rushed toward the door, eager for the freedom of the lunch period and a chance to talk and laugh with their friends.

In the crowded hallway, Esther saw Mr. Evans again. He was shoving his black bowler hat over his straight dark hair and pushing his way through the students. *Where is he going?* she wondered. The teachers usually ate with the students and made sure the children didn't get too rowdy.

"Hi, Esther. Want to eat lunch together?"

Esther turned to her fourteen-year-old sister, Anna. "Sure." She immediately forgot all about Mr. Evans.

Half an hour after lunch, the principal came into the room and whispered in Mr. Timms's ear. Esther turned to Ted again. "This is getting stranger and stranger."

Mr. Timms shook his round head as the principal left the room. With a sigh, he turned toward the class. "Will all of you please move closer together in your seats? Mr. Evans hasn't returned from lunch. His business must have taken longer than he planned. Some of his students will be joining us until he returns."

Mr. Evans's class began filing into the room as Mr. Timms finished explaining. Esther scooted closer to Ted.

"You're right," he whispered. "This *is* strange."

Esther didn't like being crowded in between Ted and the blond-haired boy from Mr. Evans's class. *It's only until Mr. Evans returns,* she reminded herself.

But Mr. Evans didn't return.

After school, Anna told them that her teacher, too, had left for lunch and not returned. "Another teacher, Miss Truman, told me that my teacher and some others went to the Farmers' and Mechanics' Bank at lunchtime. They were going to take out all the money they had at the bank."

"Why?" Esther asked. "Are they going to buy something with it?"

Anna shook her head. The brown curls so like Esther's brushed the shoulders of Anna's blue school dress. "No. They want to take their money out because they don't think the bank is a safe place to keep it anymore. Miss Truman says there's a run on the bank."

A chill shivered up Esther's spine. "A run," she repeated.

She didn't truly understand what a run was. All she knew was that she'd heard her parents and Uncle Enoch talk about runs that happened on other banks. When there were runs on banks, people who kept their money in the banks lost their savings, and people who worked at the banks lost their jobs.

"Mother and Father keep their savings at that bank," she said to Anna. "Uncle Enoch works there. Wouldn't he have told them if their money wasn't safe?"

"I'm sure he would have." Anna's voice sounded positive, but her eyes looked troubled.

Anna left to walk home with a friend, and Esther went looking for Ted. They were cousins, but they'd also been best friends all their lives. She told him what Anna had said about the bank.

Ted drew his eyebrows together in a frown beneath his red hair. "Let's go down by the bank and see whether Anna is right. Maybe it's only another rumor that there's a run on the bank."

Esther and Ted had strict orders to go straight home from school each day, but she didn't think twice before agreeing.

When they reached Fourth Street where the bank stood, they couldn't see the doors and windows of the buildings for all the people.

"We'll never get close to the bank in this crowd," Ted complained. He climbed up on a bench that stood beneath a street-lamp. "Maybe I can see what's going on from up here."

Esther climbed right up behind him. She stared in amazement. "So this is what a bank run looks like."

"Looks like a sea of men's suit coats and hats to me," Ted said. They were across the street from the bank. "There's hardly an inch of space between the people."

"I don't think the trolley car can move." Esther pointed at the top of the colorful car that stood in the middle of the street.

She didn't stare at it long. The bank was what interested her. There were three huge, round-topped archways two or three stories high across the front of the tall stone building. The entryway through the middle arch was mobbed with men.

A man with a large camera jumped up on the bench beside them. Esther gasped and grabbed the light post. Ted grabbed onto Esther with one hand and the hat covering his red hair with the other.

The man didn't seem bothered by the rocking bench. He pointed the large black box toward the bank and waited until the bench stilled. Pouf! A small black cloud appeared as he snapped his shot.

Ted peered around Esther, squinting. "You a newspaper man, mister?"

The man grinned at him and winked. "Yep. I'm a photographer for the Minneapolis *Tribune*."

"The people in the bank's doorway don't seem to be moving," Esther said. "Do you know why not?"

The photographer nodded sharply. "That's because inside the bank people are packed as solidly as they are out here in the street."

Esther looked back at the bank building. "It doesn't seem like any bank in the world could have enough money to pay all these people in one day."

The photographer grunted as he jumped down from the bench. "This one might not have enough, either. A bank down the street had a run this morning. Closed their doors at noon when they ran out of money."

Esther thought his voice sounded awfully cheerful to be telling such bad news. She watched, amazed, as the young man started off through the crowd with a bounce in his step and a whistle on his lips.

"Do you see either of our fathers?" she asked Ted.

9

He shook his head. "Not a chance of seeing them in this crowd."

"I hope they got our families' savings out. It would be awful if the bank paid out all its money before our fathers got here."

"Maybe we'd better get home and make sure they know about the run." Ted jumped down from the bench. Esther was right behind him.

They tried to hurry through the crowd, but hurrying was impossible. "I think I've said 'excuse me, please' one hundred times in the last twenty feet," Esther complained.

Ted grinned. "I quit after the first dozen. No one seemed to be paying any attention to us, anyway."

A few feet farther along, a tall man with a gray handlebar mustache stopped a younger man with a brown mustache that turned down along the sides of his wide mouth. "Hi ya, Fred. Are ya here to get yer money out of the bank?"

Fred gave his friend a grin. "Well, I came to get my money out, but a funny thing happened. I was in the lobby of the bank and feeling like a sardine squeezed into a can for all the people. Then a fellow pokes me in the arm and says, 'Mister, I'll give you fifty dollars for your place in line.' "

"Did you give it to him?" the friend asked.

"For fifty dollars? You betcha!" Fred chuckled. "I only have thirty dollars in my savings account. I figured I'd made good money for the day. I been standing in this crowd since ten this morning, trying to get into that bank. I took the fifty dollars and I'm going home."

Esther and Ted exchanged looks. Esther thought Ted looked as worried as she felt. Imagine paying someone fifty dollars just for his place in line! Things must be even worse than she'd thought.

Slowly they continued making their way through the crowd.

As they walked farther from the bank, the number of people thinned. Soon they could walk easily along the boardwalk without bumping into people.

Ted hurried across the street. Esther followed, dodging business wagons with tall white wooden covers. Names like "Hodge's Emporium," "Olsen's Meat Market," "Himmelsback's Furniture," and "Zuckerman's Dry Goods" were painted in large letters on the sides of the wagons.

"Yuck!" She jumped to one side just in time to miss a smelly pile left by one of the horses pulling a wagon.

Watching the road carefully for more piles, she caught the heel of her shoe in the rail for the trolley cars. "Oof!" She landed flat on her face in the street, her shoe still caught by the rail and her foot stuck in her shoe. She tried to push herself up but couldn't. She couldn't even breathe.

I just knocked the air out of my lungs, she thought. *I'll be all right in a minute.* She fought down her fear, trying to stay calm even though her chest and throat ached from lack of air.

Suddenly she became aware of a familiar clanging sound. A trolley car bell! She twisted her head. A trolley car was only a block away and headed right for her.

Her gaze darted toward Ted. He had reached the other side of the street and was starting down the boardwalk. He hadn't even noticed that she wasn't beside him.

She opened her mouth, gasping for air, and struggled to sit up. The clanging grew louder. She glanced in its direction. Fear spun through her. The trolley was almost on top of her!

CHAPTER 2
The Accident

From behind, strong hands grabbed her beneath her shoulders and tugged. Esther's foot wouldn't budge from the rail. "My foot!"

The bell's clang and the clatter of the wheels of the electric trolley car banged in her ears like cymbals. She turned her head away from the trolley barreling toward her. She felt a hand on her ankle. With a strong jerk, her foot was free.

"Ugh!" She heard a groan burst from the person who yanked at her arms, pulling her—almost throwing her—from the path of the trolley.

Esther could feel the wind created by the trolley car as it whizzed by. "Thank you, God," she whispered.

"Are you all right?" a boy's voice asked.

12

She looked up. A boy about her own age with straight, dark brown hair beneath a brown bicycle hat stared down at her with dark eyes. His face was tanned, but his lips looked almost white. She wondered if that was because he'd been afraid, too. "Are you. . .are you the one who helped me?" she asked in a shaky voice.

He nodded. "Are you hurt?"

Esther wasn't sure. She ached everywhere. Her ankle hurt, and she wondered whether she had twisted it. Her arms felt like they'd almost been pulled from her body when the boy grabbed her. The palms of her hands smarted from the gravel that had been driven into them when she fell. Still, she wasn't hurt so badly that she needed a doctor. "I. . .I'll be all right."

Suddenly Ted loomed over her. "Are you all right? I turned around just in time to see this guy pull you out from in front of the trolley."

"I'm all right," she repeated. She glanced up at the boy. "Thank you. I guess you about saved my life."

Ted looked at the boy with admiration shining from his eyes. "That was mighty brave of you."

The boy stood up and kicked at a pebble with the toe of a worn shoe. "Aw, it wasn't so much. Anybody would have done the same thing."

"Not anybody," Ted said. "Plenty of people wouldn't have risked their life for someone else like that, especially for someone they didn't know."

The boy held out his hand. "I'm Erik Moe."

Ted shook his hand. "Ted Fisk."

"I'm Esther Allerton, Ted's cousin."

Erik grinned. "So now we know each other, and we're not strangers anymore, so you can quit gushing all over yourselves thanking me."

They all laughed.

Esther tried to stand up, pushing against the paved street with her scraped hands. "Oooh!" Her ankle buckled, setting her down hard.

Ted and Erik both grabbed for her. "Is it your ankle?" Erik asked.

Esther nodded, holding her ankle above the buttoned shoe. She bit her bottom lip and blinked hard, trying to keep back the tears in her eyes.

"Is it broken?" Ted knelt down and tried to feel it. "Move your hand, Esther, and let me see."

Esther didn't move her hand. "I'm sure it's not broken. I think it's only twisted. It will be all right in a few minutes."

A wagon rumbled by. The horse pulling it snorted in their direction.

"You can't keep sitting in the street," Erik said. "How about if we help you over to the boardwalk?"

With one of the boys on each side of her, Esther made her way to the boardwalk, trying not to cry out at the pain in her ankle. She was glad to sit on the edge of the boardwalk with her feet in the street and lean against the bottom of a telegraph pole.

She glanced back at the tracks where she'd fallen. "My schoolbooks!"

"I'll get them." Ted hurried across the busy street. He was back in a minute with the books. "Your geography book looks all right, but I think you'll need a new arithmetic book." He held it up. The trolley's wheels had completely destroyed it.

"You should be more careful crossing the trolley tracks," Erik said.

His scolding tone embarrassed Esther. "I was watching where I was going. The heel of my shoe got caught in the track. I couldn't help that, could I?"

Ted nudged her shoulder. "If it weren't for Erik, your leg

14

would be smashed like your arithmetic book."

She wrinkled her nose at him.

Erik set down the bag he'd been carrying slung over one shoulder. He leaned against the telegraph pole and looked down at her. His brown eyes were serious. "Trolley tracks can be as dangerous as railroad tracks. You have to be careful around them. My pa worked for the railroad. He saw a lot of people hurt there. He. . .he even lost four fingers off one of his hands in an accident at the railroad yard near here."

Esther saw pain flash through Erik's eyes as he told of his father's accident. Ted exclaimed, "That's rough!" then murmured, "I'm sorry, Erik."

Hearing about Erik's father made Esther suddenly ashamed of the way she'd snapped at him a moment ago. "I'm sorry, too. You were right about the trolley tracks being dangerous. I'll be more careful after this."

"My father works for the railroad, too," Ted said. "He's an engineer for the Great Northern Railroad."

"Has he ever been hurt in an accident?" Erik asked.

Ted shook his head. "No, but I always worry about him when he's working."

Esther glanced at him in surprise. "You never told me that!"

Ted shrugged. "Lots of people are killed in railroad accidents each year, both railroad workers and passengers. Father's been in some accidents, but only small ones. No one has ever been killed on any of the trains he was driving."

"What railroad does your father work for?" Esther asked Erik. Lots of different railroad companies had stations in Minneapolis.

Erik plunged his hands into the pockets of his worn brown corduroy trousers. The wooden boardwalk thunked as he knocked the heel of his shoe against the side of it. "He doesn't work for any railroad anymore. The railroad he was with is having hard times, so they fired some of their workers. Since Pa lost all the fingers on one hand and only has a thumb left, he was one of the first people the company fired."

He kicked the boardwalk again, so hard that Esther could feel the boards beneath her bounce slightly. "He'd been with the company fifteen years, and they threw him away like a piece of garbage."

The bitterness in his voice made Esther uncomfortable.

"That's tough," Ted said again in a low voice. He cleared his throat. "Uh, what kind of accident was your father in when he lost his fingers?"

"He didn't lose all of them in one accident. He was a brakeman."

Esther and Ted glanced at each other. "It takes courage to be a brakeman," she said. Lots of brakemen lost fingers, Esther knew. Sometimes they lost entire hands or even their lives.

Erik flashed her a look of gratitude. "Pa lost two fingers in an accident three years ago, but he could still work. He lost the other two this winter."

"Was he trying to use the coupler?" Ted asked.

Erik nodded. "The last time, he was trying to attach a box-car to the train with the link-and-pin coupler. He was standing between the cars, like the brakemen always do when they're attaching cars. He was steering the iron link into the socket so he could drop in the pin that held the cars together. But the boxcar was moved at the wrong moment, and his fingers were crushed in the link-and-pin coupler."

Esther blinked back tears at the thought of what it must have been like for Erik to have his father lose his fingers. "My father is a doctor," she said. "He's seen a lot of accidents like your father's. Too many, he says."

Erik's brown eyes grew darker with anger. "Everybody says there's too many accidents, but no one does anything about it."

Ted and Esther glanced at each other but said nothing. What could they say? Erik was right.

Ted cleared his throat. "Where does your father work now?"

Erik stared at the road. "Nowhere. He hasn't been able to find a job because of the hard times." He nodded at the bag at his feet. "That's why I had to quit school and go to work as a newsboy."

Esther couldn't imagine needing to quit school to make money for her family. She knew there were children who had to do that, but she didn't know any. She thought it must be scary.

"Is your ankle feeling any better?" Erik asked.

"It still throbs," she said. "My shoe feels tighter than before."

Ted's eyebrows drew together in a frown. "That's not a good sign. Maybe your foot is swollen. Can you stand on it?"

He and Erik each took one of her arms and helped her stand. She held her breath as she put her weight on her injured foot. "Oooh!"

The boys' hands tightened on her arms.

"We'd better help you home," Ted said.

Erik nodded.

"You don't have to help, Erik," Esther said. "You have to sell your papers. I've kept you from your work too long already."

"That's all right," Erik answered. "It'll take you and Ted hours if you try to walk leaning on him."

Erik slung his bag over his shoulders. Ted put Esther's schoolbooks with his and fastened his book strap around them. Then he and Erik made a chair with their arms for Esther.

Esther still thought it took a long time to get home. The boys

17

had to stop and rest a few times along the way. The closer they got to the house, the more Esther dreaded reaching it.

She glanced down at the ruffle that ran along the bottom of her green dress, just below her knees. It dangled below the hem now. The white stocking that came up over her knee was torn, and her leg and knee were scraped like the palms of her hand. "Mother will be upset about the dress," she said to Ted.

He laughed. "You are always doing something to upset your mother."

"I bet she'll be so glad you weren't hit by the trolley car that she won't be upset at all," Erik told her.

She shook her head. "You don't know my mother. She'll say 'Esther Marie Allerton, why must you act so impulsively? Young ladies cross streets carefully and slowly. Why can't you be more like your sister, Anna?' "

Erik smiled at Esther's tone.

Ted laughed. "She sounds just like her mother," he told Erik.

Esther glanced at Erik and bit back a groan. How could she have let Erik help her home? Her parents and Ted's parents had warned them many times not to have anything to do with the city's newsboys. The adults thought the newsboys tough and were sure they would drag well-raised children into trouble.

Esther took a deep breath as the boys carried her up the front steps and across the wide wooden porch to the door of her house. Her parents weren't going to like a newsboy coming to their house with her and Ted!

CHAPTER 3
The Surprise

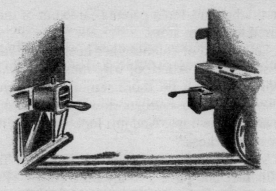

"Whatever happened to you, Esther?" Mother rushed out of the parlor and down the hallway toward the front door when the children entered the house.

"I hurt my ankle," Esther said. Ted and Erik set Esther down on one of the bottom steps of the stairway leading to the upstairs.

"I'd better go," Erik said. "See ya." He lifted a hand in a small wave and backed toward the front door. He nodded at Esther's mother, touching his fingers to the brim of his bicycle hat. "Ma'am." A second later he was outside and closing the door.

Mother frowned after him. "Have I met him before?"

"I don't think so," Ted said. "We just met him today."

Esther groaned and darted Ted a sharp glance. Surely he knew better than to say that! Her mother was going to be upset enough when she discovered Erik was a newsboy.

"Where did you meet him?" Mother asked.

"When I hurt my ankle." Esther leaned down and rubbed her ankle, groaning slightly.

As she'd hoped, her mother forgot about Erik instantly. She knelt in front of Esther and began unbuttoning the shoe. "What happened?"

Esther's father and Ted's parents came out of the parlor as Esther started to tell the story.

When Esther told of catching her heel on the rail, Mother sighed. "Esther Marie Allerton, why must you act so impulsively? Why can't you be more feminine, like your sister, Anna? Young ladies cross streets slowly and cautiously. They don't race across like boys. And just look what you did to your pretty new school dress."

Esther glanced at Ted and tried not to groan. Ted put his fist up to his face and gave a funny little cough. Esther knew he was trying not to laugh. She looked away to keep from laughing herself and continued her story.

When she told of Erik pulling her to safety, her mother asked, "Is that the boy who came home with you?"

Esther nodded. "He probably saved my life, or at least my leg."

"Yes, he probably did," her father said, kneeling in front of her. "We'll have to thank him properly." He ran experienced fingers lightly over her ankle. "Swollen but not broken. It will likely hurt for a few days. I'll bandage it so it will be easier to walk on. Marcia," he turned to his wife, "could you get some ice? It might be too late to help the swelling, but we can try it."

Mother hurried down the hallway and through a swinging

20

door into the kitchen.

Father helped Esther into the parlor, where she sat in his favorite stuffed chair covered in green velvet and rested her foot on a matching footstool. In a few minutes, Mother was back with a chunk of ice wrapped in a linen towel.

Esther flinched when her father set the cold towel on her ankle. "It will help," he said, holding it in place.

Mother stood behind him, shaking her head.

Ted's mother came to stand beside her. "Tell us more about this brave lad who helped you."

Esther was glad Aunt Alison had changed the subject from Esther's shortcomings, though she was sure her mother wouldn't think Erik so brave when she discovered he was a newsboy. She wished her own mother were more like Aunt Alison. Her aunt never got as upset as her mother over the small scrapes Esther and Ted's impulsive acts got them into.

Before she could say anything, Ted jumped in eagerly and told how Erik had risked his own safety to help Esther.

"I wish he would have stayed so we could thank him in person," Mother said.

Esther glanced at her in pleased surprise. "He's very nice."

"Even though he is a newsboy," Ted added.

Mother's face swung toward Ted. "A newsboy?"

Esther leaned her head against the back of the chair and closed her eyes.

"What were you two doing with a newsboy?" Mother asked.

Ted fidgeted, shifting his weight from one foot to the other. "We weren't with him when Esther fell. We didn't even know him until afterward. He helped Esther even though he didn't know her."

"That was brave and honorable of him," Esther's father said, "but you know we don't want you making friends with newsboys."

"Yes, sir," Esther muttered.

"That goes for you, too, Theodore," Aunt Alison said.

"Yes, ma'am," Ted muttered.

"Erik isn't a newsboy because he wants to be one," Esther told their parents. "He has to work because his father lost his job."

"That's right," Ted added from his seat in a tall-backed oak rocking chair on the other side of the room. He told how Erik's father lost his fingers and then his job.

"It's terrible that men like Erik's father have had to lose their fingers and their lives doing their jobs," Uncle Charles agreed. "About twenty-five years ago, when I was younger than you, a man named Eli Hamilton Janney invented a new kind of coupler to connect railroad cars. It automatically connects, or couples, the cars when the cars are pushed together. It's much safer than the old way."

Ted's almost-black eyes flashed. "Then why don't the railroads use the new coupler?"

"The railroad companies thought it was too expensive to add to the railroad cars. Only the Pennsylvania Railroad used it. They thought it worked well. Then a few years ago, Iowa made a law that all railroads in Iowa had to use both Janney's coupler and a safer kind of brake called an air brake."

Esther sat up straighter. Anger, more powerful than the pain in her ankle, swirled through her chest. "I think it's *awful* railroads are more worried about money than about people like Erik's father! Why don't all railroads in all the states have to use the safest brakes and couplers?"

"Soon they will," Uncle Charles said. "The United States has a new organization called the Interstate Commerce Commission. It makes rules for companies that do business in more than one state. This spring they made a rule saying all railroads have to use Janney's coupler and the air brake."

"Hurrah!" Ted leaped to his feet. The chair rocked like a boat on one of Minnesota's wind-blown lakes.

His mother raised her eyebrows and shook her head. "Theodore, don't let the chair hit the wall."

Although Aunt Alison's words sounded like scolding and the children always knew she was serious when she called him Theodore, Esther could hear a laugh behind her aunt's voice.

While Ted slowed the chair's rocking and sat down again, Esther said, "I'm glad about the new rule, Uncle Charles, but the rule came too late for Erik's father."

"Yes," he admitted, "and that's a shame. But he probably helped get the new rule passed."

"How could he do that?" Ted asked.

"Yes, how?" Esther repeated. "He was only a brakeman, not a rich man."

"The brakemen have a union. Through the union, the brakemen work together to try to get railroads to do things in ways that make their work safer. The brakemen's union told the Interstate Commerce Commission how safe Janney's coupler is."

Ted frowned. "Is the brakemen's union like the railroad engineers' union that you belong to, Father?"

Uncle Charles nodded. "Yes. There's lots of different unions. There's a plumbers' union, and a carpenters' union, and a tailors' union. Each one tries to make working conditions better for their own kind of jobs."

"There are unions that try to help all working people, too, no matter what their jobs," Father told them, looking up from Esther's ankle, which he'd just finished wrapping in a bandage. "One is called the Knights of Labor. Another is the American Federation of Labor, which most people call the AFL."

"I've heard of them," Esther said.

Uncle Charles smiled at her. "In addition to trying to make work safer, they try to get better wages for their members—

and shorter work hours. Those are some of the reasons your brother Walter thinks unions are so important, Ted."

Ted grinned. "Walter is always talking about unions and going to union meetings."

Father stood up. "Better wages and shorter hours are nice for the working men, but I think that helping make things safer is the most important work they do. I suppose that's because I'm a doctor and treat so many people hurt in unnecessary accidents. Some bosses make things as safe as they can for their workers without laws, but not all."

"That's right," Uncle Charles agreed. "The new law about couplers and air brakes will make trains safer for both workers and the people riding the trains. About 6,400 people were killed in railroad accidents last year, and almost 30,000 were injured."

"Wow!" Esther stared at Ted. His eyes were as big as hers felt. "No wonder the new rule was made."

"Sometimes people have to see how bad things are before they do something to change them," Father said.

"Erik's father isn't the only railroad man to lose his job this year," Uncle Charles said. "A number of railroads are declaring bankruptcy. They owe more money than they can make."

Ted stared at him. "Is. . .is your railroad in trouble?"

Ted's voice sounded high and tight. Esther felt suddenly sick to her stomach. Would Uncle Charles lose his job? What if Ted had to quit school and go to work like Erik?

Uncle Charles shook his head. "The Great Northern Railroad is in good shape. James Hill is too good a businessman to let the company get in trouble."

Esther's stomach felt instantly better, and she saw a grin on Ted's face. The she remembered the bank run. She sat up with a jerk that bumped her sore ankle against the shoe on her other foot. She winced but ignored her pain in order to deliver her message. "We almost forgot to tell you why Ted and I were in such a hurry on our way home."

She and Ted interrupted each other again and again telling the story of the bank run.

"Have you talked to Uncle Enoch?" Ted asked when they were done.

"No," said Uncle Charles.

"No," Father added, "but—"

"Maybe you should take your money out of the bank and put it somewhere safe," Esther interrupted.

Father and Uncle Charles exchanged looks. "I think we'll wait until we talk with Enoch," Uncle Charles said slowly.

Father nodded.

Esther thought it looked like there was something almost like fright in their eyes, but she wasn't sure. She'd never seen any of their parents afraid before.

"But. . ." She licked her lips. Her parents usually didn't take advice from their children. She took a deep breath and started again. "What if all the bank's money is gone by the time you talk to Uncle Enoch? There were a lot of people there."

Ted sat on the edge of the rocker and nodded.

"I'm sure Enoch would have told us if our money wasn't safe," Father said with a small smile.

Is that a true smile, Esther wondered, *or a smile to make me and Ted feel better?*

Ted rubbed his hands over his knees. "Esther's right. You should talk to Uncle Enoch right away."

"We will, Son," Uncle Charles said. "We promise."

"Enoch and his wife are joining us for dinner this evening," Mother said. "Your fathers can ask him about the bank then."

Esther and Ted glanced at each other. She wasn't at all sure that would be soon enough.

Aunt Alison stood up. "I'm tired of all this dreary talk. I

25

think we could all use a dose of something more cheerful. Ted, Esther, I think Esther's parents have a surprise for you."

Esther looked at her mother expectantly.

"A surprise?" Ted's grin grew.

Father went to stand beside the dainty upholstered chair where Mother sat beside the fireplace doing needlework. He put his hand on her shoulder and asked, "What do you think? Should we tell them yet or make them wait?"

Mother put her needlework down and leaned her head to one side. She looked at Ted, then at Esther. "I'm not so sure. Perhaps they've had enough excitement for one day."

Esther could see her father's eyes sparkling with mischief. Excitement bubbled inside her. "Tell us now!"

Father laughed. "How would you two like to go to the fair?"

Esther frowned. "The state fair? That's not until fall."

Mother smiled.

Father shook his head. "Not the state fair. The World's Fair. The Columbian Exposition in Chicago."

CHAPTER 4

An Unexpected Meeting

"The World's Fair? Oh, yes!" Esther grabbed the arms of the green velvet chair and pushed her feet from the footstool to stand up. "Ooooh!" She sank back down.

"Whoopee!" Ted leaped from his chair. It banged against the wall.

"Theodore!" Aunt Alison's voice held a sterner tone than usual. "If you let that chair hit the wall one more time, you will have to repaint and paper your aunt and uncle's parlor before you go to the fair, if we allow you to go at all."

Ted grabbed the arms of the chair, stopping it. "Yes, Mother." He couldn't stop grinning, though. He knew his mother would never keep him away from something as important as the

27

World's Fair. "When do we leave?"

"Not until after school lets out for the summer," Uncle Charles said.

Ted pretended to be disappointed.

Father laughed. "Besides, we have to wait until Esther's ankle is better. We'll be doing lots of walking at the fair. It's as big as a small town."

"Are Richard and Anna going, too?" Esther asked. It would be more fun with her sixteen-year-old brother and fourteen-year-old sister along. She was glad when Father said they would be going.

While their mothers prepared dinner and their fathers read the evening newspaper, Ted sat on the large velvet-covered footstool beside Esther, and they made plans for their trip. They were so excited about it that they completely forgot about Uncle Enoch and the bank run.

When Uncle Enoch and Aunt Tina arrived for dinner an hour later, Esther and Ted looked at each other. They both remembered the bank run.

Aunt Tina went into the kitchen with the other women. Uncle Enoch hung his stylish black bowler hat on the hat rack beside the other men's hats. Then he went to speak with Ted and Esther's fathers.

The men were across the room from Ted and Esther. They spoke in such low voices that the children could only hear a few words. The cousins stopped talking and tried to hear the men.

"We won't be able to take the trip if our fathers lose all their money," Esther whispered.

Ted didn't answer.

Finally Uncle Charles looked over toward them. "You two may as well hear what your uncle Enoch has to say, since you already know about the bank run."

The men moved closer so Esther wouldn't have to move with her sore ankle.

Uncle Enoch sat on the edge of the small beige chair with pink roses that Mother had sat on while doing her needlework. He looked very big on such a dainty chair, but it was the closest chair to Esther.

He leaned forward with an elbow on his good knee. The jacket of his business suit hung open. "The Farmers' and Mechanics' Bank, where I work, has more than enough money to pay all the people who keep their savings there." He held up his right hand, palm out. "I give you my word: your parents' money is safe."

Esther wanted to believe him, but it was hard after seeing all those people at the bank earlier. She was glad when Ted asked, "Then why was there a run on your bank?"

Uncle Enoch spread his hands and lifted his eyebrows. "We aren't certain, but we have an idea. We think people mixed us up with another bank. The Farmers' and Merchants' Bank sounds a lot like my bank, the Farmers' and Mechanics' Bank, doesn't it?"

The two cousins nodded.

"Well," Uncle Enoch continued, "the other bank—the Farmers' and Merchants' Bank—had a run on it this morning. That bank hadn't as much money as we do in our vaults. They locked their doors at noon because they didn't have any more money to pay to the people who kept their savings at that bank."

"Why doesn't the bank have the people's money?" Esther asked.

"Yes, why?" Ted repeated. "When people put money in the bank, isn't the bank supposed to put their money in the vault to keep it safe until the people want it back?"

"Not exactly." Uncle Enoch pushed his round, wire-rimmed

glasses into place. "When people put their money in the bank, they are called depositors. The bank pays depositors interest for putting their money in the bank."

Ted and Esther nodded.

"Why do you think the bank pays people for bringing their money to the bank?" Uncle Enoch asked.

Esther shook her head. "I don't know."

Ted frowned. "I don't know, either."

Uncle Enoch smiled. "The bank pays people interest for letting the bank use their money."

Surprise jerked Ted up straight. "You mean the bank doesn't keep the money in the safe?"

"Not all of it," Uncle Enoch said. "Much of it is loaned to people and businesses."

"Like when a man needs a loan to build a house?" Ted asked.

"Yes." Uncle Enoch smiled. "Or when a businessman needs a loan to add on to his business. When the bank loans someone money, *they* pay the *bank* interest."

"I see now!" Ted threw his hands in the air. "It's simple. The people with the loans pay the bank interest. Then the bank uses that money to pay interest to the depositors."

"That's right," Uncle Enoch agreed.

"I understand now," Esther said.

Uncle Enoch leaned forward to explain more. "When there's a run on a bank, like there was on our bank and the other bank today, it doesn't cause any trouble if the bank hasn't loaned out too much money. Understand?"

Ted and Esther nodded.

"What happens to the depositors who wanted to take their money back out of the other bank but couldn't get it today?" Ted asked.

"That depends," Uncle Enoch said. "If the people the bank

30

loaned the money to pay it back, the bank can pay the depositors, but not right away."

"What if the people with the loans don't pay back the bank?" Ted asked slowly.

"Then the depositors might lose their savings," Uncle Enoch said soberly.

"Are you sure the people *your* bank loaned money to will pay it back?"

Uncle Enoch nodded. "We believe most of them will. We're very careful about who we lend our depositors' money to."

"I hope so," Esther said, pointing a finger at Uncle Enoch and wiggling it playfully, "because I want to go to the World's Fair in Chicago!"

Ted and the men laughed. "Me, too," her father said, his eyes sparkling with laughter.

Ted and Esther hoped to leave for the fair as soon as school was out for the summer, but that didn't happen. They grew restless waiting for the end of July, when Father said they would leave.

In the meantime, they read everything they could find on the fair. The Minneapolis *Tribune* had many articles about it. Esther's brother and sister, Richard and Anna, and Esther's parents read the articles as eagerly as Ted and Esther. They spent many evenings in the Allerton parlor planning their trip and which exhibits each most wanted to see.

"Can't we leave this week?" Esther asked at the end of one such evening. "This waiting is terrible. Why, I'm going to be an old maid before we get there!"

Everyone laughed.

Mother smiled primly. "Planning a trip is half the fun."

Esther and Ted exchanged exasperated looks.

Esther sighed and flopped down on her stomach in the

middle of the flowered parlor rug, her arms folded across the newspaper where she had been reading about Minnesota's building at the fair.

"Do sit up, Esther," Mother said, shaking her head. "I wonder if I shall ever make a young lady of you. If you continue to flop around on the floor like a boy, you may be an old maid one day after all."

Esther sat up, the corners of her lips bent down and her cheeks red.

"At least there's the Hill parade later this week," Ted reminded Esther.

"Yes." Esther smiled at him, grateful that her cousin was trying to ease her embarrassment.

The parade was to celebrate the arrival of James Hill's Great Northern Railroad at Puget Sound on the Pacific coast. James Hill had started out as a young man in St. Paul, the sister city of Minneapolis. The two cities thought his accomplishment was their accomplishment, too.

"It sounds like the parade is going to be gigantic," Richard said. "One of the biggest affairs ever held in the Twin Cities."

"It should be." Father's newspaper crackled as he lowered it and looked at them over the top of it. "Mr. Hill is thought by many to be the greatest man in the United States."

"Not by Uncle Enoch," Esther reminded him. "Uncle Enoch thinks Mr. Hill takes foolish risks with his money."

Ted laughed. "He has a lot of money to take risks with. The newspaper says he has twenty-five million dollars."

"Someone with that much money could never go broke," Esther said.

Ted nodded, smiling.

Richard rested his elbows on his knees and spread his hands. "Still, hundreds of railroads are going broke this year. The panic is causing money trouble everywhere. And it must have cost James Hill a lot of money to build the railroad all the way from Minnesota to Puget Sound."

"People did call it Hill's Folly," Father agreed.

Esther glanced at Ted and noticed a frown on his face. Was he afraid that the Great Northern Railroad could be in trouble? What would happen to Ted if Uncle Charles lost his job?

That Saturday, Ted went to the railroad yard to meet his father and walk home from work with him. As he headed toward the yard, he remembered the conversation at the Allertons'. His stomach tightened. Angrily he pushed the scary thoughts away.

"Hey, there! Ted! Wait up!"

Ted turned at the call, glad to see Erik running toward him across the wooden platform in front of the station house. He dodged through the people who were always streaming from the large station. Erik carried his bicycle hat in one hand, and his straight brown hair flopped as he ran. A grin spread across his friendly face.

Ted grinned back. "What are you doing here? Shouldn't you be working?"

"I've sold all my papers. The railroad station is always a good place to sell them. People arriving want the latest news. People leaving want something to read on the train." He fell into step beside Ted. "What are you doing here?"

"I'm meeting my father." Ted hesitated. He didn't want to seem unfriendly, but he remembered his parents' warnings not to become friendly with newsboys. *If they knew Erik, maybe they'd like him,* he thought. "Would. . .would you like to come along and meet him?"

"Sure!"

Ted had been sure Erik would want to meet his father. Most boys he knew wanted to meet him. Engineers had exciting, good-paying jobs. Many men started work on the railroad as brakemen, like Erik's father. Even though the job was dangerous, the men did it in hopes of one day becoming an important engineer.

The boys stopped to watch a train steaming into the station. Ted held his breath while a brakeman ran across the top of the railroad cars and grabbed the round wheel at the back of a car. The man braced himself and turned the wheel to brake the car. The train slowed. Steam hissed from behind the wheels.

Ted grinned at Erik. "Your father must be brave to have been a brakeman. Running across the top of the cars looks exciting, but I wouldn't want to do it at night or in a snowstorm or when a train is flying down the track at forty miles an hour."

Erik didn't smile back. "I'll be glad when the trains all have the new air brakes. Then engineers like your father will be able to stop the trains safely from the engine."

Ted didn't know what to say.

When they reached Ted's father's engine, the train's fireman was holding a large copper can with a long skinny spout. Ted knew he was using it to oil the bearings on the drive wheels, which were taller than the fireman.

"Hello, Mr. Thomas," Ted said, touching his fingers to his baseball hat. "Have a good trip?"

"Yup. Glad to be back, though."

Mr. Thomas's face was red and wrinkled. It seemed to Ted that the man's face was always red. He supposed it was from shoveling coal to make steam for the engine hour after hour during the train trips. It was one of his duties to make sure the train was kept in safe running condition, too. The safety of the passengers depended on Mr. Thomas doing his work well.

Through the engine's side window, Ted saw his father. "Hello, Father!"

Father turned and waved, smiling. Ted saw his gaze dart to Erik, then back. His smile went away. "I'll be with you in a minute," he called.

Ted pushed his hands into the pockets of his brown knickers. He didn't want Erik to see how nervous he was. What if his father was angry at him for being with Erik? Would he tell Erik to go away? He hoped not. Erik was a nice boy. Ted didn't want his feelings or his pride hurt.

Ted could see his father was talking with another train worker. He turned to Erik. "Did you see the parade Wednesday?"

Erik nodded and laughed. "There wasn't any reason to be anywhere else. I think all of Minneapolis and St. Paul were there."

"My family and Esther's were there, too. Wasn't it great?"

"Sure was. What was your favorite part of the parade?" Erik asked.

"All the different kinds of transportation: the Indians with their horse-drawn drag, the voyageurs in their canoe, the dogsled, the Red River Cart with its two large, solid wooden wheels—"

Erik's laugh interrupted him. "Did you ever hear anything as awful as those wheels screeching? I bet when those carts crossed the prairie, you could hear them for miles."

"The wheels could have used Mr. Thomas's oilcan, that's certain," Ted agreed. "Let's see, what came next? Oh, yes. The model of the first steamboat that came up the Mississippi. Then the prairie schooner, with the two cows tied behind and the stovepipe sticking out the back."

"My father remembers seeing them a lot when he was young," Erik said. "He called them covered wagons."

"My father, too. Then came the stagecoach." Ted shook his head. "Hard to believe there are still parts of the country where people can't travel on trains, isn't it?"

"Must be awful slow traveling any other way," Erik agreed.

Just then, Father came down from the engine to greet the boys.

"This is Erik Moe, Father," Ted said. He clasped his hands behind his back, hoping they weren't shaking. Would his father like Erik, or would he be rude to him? "Erik is the newsboy who helped Esther when she tripped on the trolley rails."

"It's nice to meet you, Mr. Fisk," Erik said.

Father hesitated. His gaze seemed to study Erik's face. Then he held out his large, calloused hand. "A pleasure to meet you, Erik. Your bravery saved my niece's leg, if not her life."

Erik shrugged, his shoulders lifting his worn, once-white shirt. "Anyone would have done the same, sir."

Ted's breath came out in a "whoosh" of relief.

Before Father could reply, a booming voice came from behind Ted and Erik. "Why, it's Mr. Fisk, isn't it? Charles Fisk."

Ted turned around and looked at the man with the cheerful voice. The man was stout, with a chest that looked like a barrel covered by a fine tailored suit jacket. The top of his head was bald, but the hair on the sides of his head was so long that it almost touched the collar of his double-breasted jacket. In one hand he held a stovepipe hat. A full, neatly trimmed beard and moustache covered his chin and lower face.

Ted's jaw dropped. "James Hill!"

CHAPTER 5
Mr. Hill's Story

"Ted, mind your manners," Father scolded in a low voice. Gulping, Ted closed his mouth.

Mr. Hill looked Ted in the eye. He held out his hand. "James Hill it is. I came down to look over my trains. And you are?"

Ted shook his hand. "Ted. . .that is, Theodore Fisk, sir." He knew that Mr. Hill lived in a grand house in St. Paul, but he certainly had never expected to meet the great man.

"Ah, then you must be Charles's son." Mr. Hill looked at Erik. "And is this another of your boys?"

Father shook his head. "No, sir. This is a friend of my son's, Erik Moe."

Mr. Hill shook hands solemnly with Erik, then held out his hand to Father. "A pleasure to see you again. Glad to see you are working for my railroad now. You were working for another line years ago, when we met."

Ted swallowed his surprise. His father had never told him he'd met the famous railroad builder!

"I'm surprised you recall our meeting," Father said. "It was many years ago."

A smile gleamed in the midst of Mr. Hill's graying mustache and beard. "Many years ago, but I always remember men who love the railroad as much as I do."

Ted saw the pleasure in his father's eyes. "I remember you took over your first railroad in 1879, only three years after I moved here from Cincinnati."

Mr. Hill nodded. "Wonderful years, those were. Minneapolis wasn't much more than a frontier town then. Only about 35,000 people. Now it's a true city, with 167,000 people."

Father smiled. "In large part due to the railroads and men of vision, such as yourself."

"And men like you. Without good engineers and other railroad workers, my dreams could never have been realized."

"My dad worked for a railroad," Erik said. Ted glanced at him and saw his chin jut out in an angry, proud manner. "He was a brakeman. He lost his fingers, and now he's out of work."

Mr. Hill's sharp eyes stared at Erik a minute. Then he rested a hand on Erik's shoulder. "I'm sorry, son. Did he work for the Great Northern?"

"No."

"Has he found other work?" Mr. Hill asked.

"No."

Ted watched uneasily. How had Erik dared speak so angrily to such an important man? He watched Mr. Hill study Erik's face.

"Are you helping support the family then, Erik?"

Erik crossed his arms over his chest and glared at Mr. Hill. "Yes. I had to quit school and find a job. I'm a newsboy. Some of us aren't as lucky as you."

Mr. Hill's head jerked in surprise. "Lucky, is it? Don't you know that luck is only another name for hard work? Let me tell you a little about my life. We're not so different as you think."

Erik snorted.

Ted swallowed a groan. Father was glaring at Erik. He would never let Ted be friends with Erik after this!

"I was born in Canada," the great man began. "I went to school from the age of seven until I was fifteen. Then my father died, and I had to leave school."

Surprise pushed the anger from Erik's eyes. "I. . .I'm sorry. I didn't know."

Mr. Hill once again put a hand on Erik's shoulder. "Never stop learning just because you've quit school. Over the years, I've gathered enough books to have my own library. And I listen to others who are more knowledgeable than I am."

Erik nodded.

"I always loved travel," Mr. Hill continued, "so when I was eighteen, I left home and came to St. Paul. There were no railroads crossing Minnesota then, but goods had to be taken between Winnipeg, Canada, on the Red River and St. Paul on the Mississippi River."

"I bet I know how the goods were transported," Ted said. "By those screeching old Red River carts."

Mr. Hill threw back his head and laughed. "You've described the carts well. And you are correct. Goods traveled by Red River carts and by steamships. I wanted to find a better way. So in the middle of winter, I took a dogsled and traveled across country. Only Indians, fur traders, and missionaries lived in that part of Minnesota then."

"Dogsled!" Ted leaned forward. "That sounds exciting!"

"Don't interrupt, Ted," his father reminded him quietly.

Mr. Hill smiled at him. "It was exciting, but mostly it was cold."

Ted laughed. He decided he quite liked this man.

"I and some friends bought a small, struggling railroad," Mr. Hill continued, "and laid lines across Minnesota from St. Paul to the Red River. It took us ten years. That was the beginning of my transportation business. Later I had bigger dreams."

"Like the Great Northern line from St. Paul to Puget Sound, Hill's Folly," Ted said.

"Ted!" Father roared.

Ted clasped a hand over his mouth. How could he have repeated that awful name for Mr. Hill's railroad? He slipped the hand from his face. "I'm sorry, sir. I didn't mean to. . .to. . ."

"I've heard others call my plan a folly," Mr. Hill said calmly. "Although other railroads had been built across the country to the West Coast, no one had ever built one without the government giving them the land. People thought that was the only way a railroad could be built, because it takes so much land."

"But you did it," Ted said. "And you had to cross the mountains, too."

Mr. Hill smiled. "Yes. I see you know a bit about my railroad."

Ted shrugged his shoulders, feeling embarrassed and pleased at the same time. "My father has told me a lot about it."

Mr. Hill folded his hands over his chest. "Let me tell you about crossing the mountains. It's difficult to build a railroad over a tall mountain, you know."

Ted and Erik nodded.

Mr. Hill brushed dirt from the iron step leading to the engine's cab. Mr. Thomas jumped forward, whisking a large red handkerchief from his back pocket. "Let me do that for ya, sir. You'll be gettin' yer hands dirty."

"I've been dirty lots of times before," Hill said, but he let Mr. Thomas wipe the step. "Thank you, sir," he said, sitting down.

"You were going to tell us about the mountains," Ted reminded him.

"Well, when the Great Northern's line neared the Rocky Mountains, I remembered a lost pass I'd heard about years ago."

"Lost pass?" Erik repeated breathlessly.

Mr. Hill nodded, his long, trim beard rubbing the front of his shirt and jacket. "Indians had told of a low point between the mountains that their people used. No one had used the pass in over forty years, so no one knew for sure where it was."

"What did you do?" Erik asked.

"I sent my chief engineer, John Stevens, to find it. It took him weeks and weeks, but at last he succeeded. He crossed the Divide on snowshoes. Then he started back. It was very cold. He couldn't sleep that night because he was afraid he'd go to sleep in the cold and never wake up."

"Why didn't he build a fire?" Erik asked. "Weren't there any trees? Didn't he have any matches?"

"There were trees and he had matches. But the snow was too deep to build a fire."

Ted and Erik stared at each other. They both knew what very cold weather felt like. The temperature was often below zero in Minneapolis. But Ted couldn't imagine there being too much snow to build a fire. "What did Mr. Stevens do?" he asked.

"He walked all night to keep from falling asleep. He went back and forth on the same path, so he wouldn't get lost in the dark. In the morning, he went down the mountain to his camp. The pass is called the Marais Pass because the Marais River

41

runs through it. Mr. Stevens's brave work shortened the Great Northern route by one hundred miles."

"Wow!" Ted shook his head.

"We weren't done with the mountains yet," Hill continued. "We still had to get over the Cascades."

"Aren't they the mountains near Puget Sound?" Ted asked.

"Very good!" Hill congratulated. "They are indeed."

"Did you have to find another lost pass through them?" Erik asked.

"No, but it was hard work. Stevens looked for the best way over the Cascades. I wanted to be sure I agreed with his plan, so I took the Northern Pacific Railroad as close as I could."

Ted and Erik and the railway men laughed at the thought of Mr. Hill using his competitors' train.

Mr. Hill smiled. "Then I took a buckboard and went to look over Stevens's planned route. I took my own bedding and slept out under the stars or stopped at the engineers' camps. Had to give up the wagon when I came to the Cascades. Went through them on horseback."

Erik shifted his feet. "I guess you meant it when you said luck is hard work."

Hill winked at him.

"Are the trees in Washington as large as the one in the parade yesterday?" Erik asked.

Ted remembered the log Seattle had sent to the parade. It was only a piece of a pine tree, but he'd never seen one so big around. It was on a large wooden flat wagon pulled by four strong horses. A man sat on the top—a logger, Ted guessed. He'd looked like an ant on top of that big log.

"The trees are truly that big," Hill told him.

"Why did you want to build the Great Northern all the way to Seattle," Erik asked, "when there were other railroads already at the Pacific?"

"Because of the trees you asked about," Hill said. "The trees have been sent by ships to other parts of the country. But people between Minnesota and the Rocky Mountains need trees to build houses and farms and towns. A railroad is the quickest way to get the trees to the people. Many people haven't moved to these lands because they don't have lumber."

"I hadn't thought of that," Ted said.

"And there's the farmers' crops. They have to get them to market. The flour mills in Minneapolis wouldn't employ so many men if farmers couldn't get their wheat to the mills to be ground into flour."

Mr. Hill took a deep breath and let it out. "The Great Northern. Hill's Folly. People have laughed at a lot of things I wanted to do—said they couldn't be done. But I've done them. Never let people tell you that you can't do the things you dream. Do you have a dream, Ted?"

Ted shook his head. "I don't know what I want to be yet. There're so many things to choose from."

"What about you, Erik?" the man asked.

Erik looked at the worn toes of his shoes. "I want to be. . . I want to be a newspaper reporter, but I guess that'll never happen. Not when I had to quit school."

Ted glanced at his friend in surprise. Erik hadn't mentioned his dream before. He wondered if Erik had ever told anyone about it.

"Believe in your dreams and a way will open," Mr. Hill told him. He bounced a thick index finger in front of Erik's face. "But don't think they will happen without lots of hard work. Do you read the newspapers you sell?"

"Every day," Erik answered promptly.

"That's good. Do you know what makes a news story good?"

"I. . .I'm not sure. I think so."

"I'm interviewed by lots of reporters," Mr. Hill told him.

43

"You asked good questions when I told you about building the Great Northern line."

Erik smiled.

"Ask some of the reporters at the newspaper you work for how to write a good story," Mr. Hill suggested.

"Yes, sir," Erik said. Ted thought Erik didn't look like he believed there was any chance he'd ever be a reporter.

"What is your father's name and what railroad did he work for?" Mr. Hill asked Erik.

Erik told him. Mr. Hill nodded, then turned his attention to Ted's father. The two men spent a few minutes talking about the Great Northern and then Mr. Hill went on his way.

When the important man had gone, Ted asked his father, "Do you believe what he said about dreams?"

"Well, the Bible says that God gives us the desires of our hearts. I believe God can put desires in our hearts to show us what He wants us to do with our lives. I certainly believe that making our dreams come true takes hard work."

Ted looked at him thoughtfully. "When you were a boy, you had a dream of working on the railroad, didn't you?"

"Yes."

"Your dream came true."

"Yes, with a lot of hard work. It wouldn't have come true if I had gone into some other kind of work." Father stepped into the engine for a last look around, then jumped to the ground. "Ready to go home?"

Ted walked alongside his father and Erik. His father had had a dream when he was Ted's age. Erik had a dream, too. *Will I ever have a dream?* he wondered.

CHAPTER 6
The Adventure Begins

Ted entered the huge station house with his parents. His ears filled with the rumble of waiting trains, the calls of conductors hurrying passengers aboard, and the clattering of wheels as porters dashed about with luggage.

Ted and his parents tried to locate Esther's family in the crowd. Ted noticed a girl jumping up and down. Brown curls flowed over her shoulders beneath a straw hat. She was helping the hat pins keep the hat in place with one gloved hand as she bounced. With the other hand, she waved furiously.

Ted laughed as he recognized his cousin. "There they are," he told his parents. He hurried across the large room.

Esther grabbed his hands, squeezing them. "Isn't it wonderful? I thought the end of July would never come! We're going to the fair! We're going to the fair!" She started jumping up and down again.

Ted laughed. "Your eyes are as big as your hat!"

"Esther Marie Allerton," her mother said in a prim voice. "Stop leaping around like a. . .a toad and behave yourself."

Esther whirled about. "But it's so exciting, Mother!"

"Try to be excited in a more ladylike manner." Esther's mother folded her gloved hands in front of her waist.

"Yes, Mother," Esther murmured. She glanced at Ted and rolled her eyes.

"That dark green dress brings out your pretty green eyes," Ted's mother said to Esther. "Is it new?"

"Yes." Esther beamed a smile and turned all the way around to show off her outfit. "I love the leg-o'-mutton sleeves with the huge puffs at the shoulders, don't you, Aunt Alison?"

"They're lovely," she agreed. "I like the huge lace collar, too."

"I wanted new shoes," Esther told her, lowering her voice and glancing over at her mother to be sure she wasn't overheard. "But Mother said new shoes would only give me blisters at the fair."

"I'm sure she's right," her aunt replied. "The newspaper articles say that a person would have to walk 150 miles to see everything at the fair."

Ted laughed. "I guess your mother was right, Esther."

Esther joined in his laughter. "I have another new dress, too," she said, "and so does Anna."

Ted ran a finger beneath the stiff starched collar of his white linen shirt. "Mother insisted on buying me new clothes, too. Wish she hadn't."

His mother and Esther laughed together at him, but he was

46

serious. "Old clothes are always more comfortable," he said, yanking at the too-tight buttons below the knees on his navy blue knickers.

"Do you have a new traveling satchel, too?" Esther asked. "Mother bought me this red one." She pointed to the bag at her feet.

Ted shrugged one shoulder, scratching at his neck where the new collar bothered him. "I'm using one of Father's old ones."

Esther's father turned from the porter who was loading their larger bags onto his cart. "Anything else that goes in the baggage car?"

Her mother shook her head. "I believe we'll need all the smaller bags on the sleeper car tonight."

Uncle Enoch and Aunt Tina walked up while Esther's father tipped the porter.

"How nice of you to see us off!" her mother said to them. "I only wish you and Ted's parents were coming with us."

Ted's father shook his head. "Train tickets are $16.30 each. Then there's the cost of the hotel and food and tickets to the fair and the special exhibits. The tickets to enter the fair are fifty cents per person! Too much in these hard times for a poor railroad engineer."

A sliver of fear slipped up Ted's spine. There was a teasing grin on his father's face, but his voice sounded serious. "I thought the Great Northern wasn't in any danger of going bankrupt," Ted said. "I mean, with Mr. Hill so rich and everything. . ." His voice trailed off.

Father squeezed his shoulder and smiled. "Mr. Hill is a good businessman. The railroad is in fine shape."

Ted wanted to believe him. He hadn't thought to wonder before this why his parents weren't going to the fair. Was his father afraid of losing his job?

47

Uncle Enoch leaned on his cane to take the pressure off his one good leg. "The Northern Pacific Railroad has gone bankrupt."

Ted darted a scared glance at Uncle Enoch. The Northern Pacific had reached the Pacific Ocean at Portland about ten years before James Hill's railroad reached Seattle. If that huge railroad couldn't make money, how could the Great Northern?

"James Hill is planning to buy the Northern Pacific," Uncle Enoch continued, "and join it with his Great Northern Railroad."

Father laughed. "And you thought Hill was foolish to build the Great Northern across the continent."

Uncle Enoch didn't join in Father's laughter. "Hill hasn't paid for the Northern Pacific yet, and the panic isn't over. A lot of railroads have gone under. Hill's roads may, too."

Esther grinned up at him. "At least you were right about your bank, Uncle Enoch. Our fathers' money is safe, and we're going to the fair!"

"That you are." Uncle Enoch winked at her.

"But the other bank you told us about closed," Ted added. "Its depositors lost their money, didn't they?"

Uncle Enoch nodded.

"Boarding for Chicago! Boarding for Chicago!" A uniformed boy a little older than Richard passed by.

Excitement pushed away Ted's fears. Esther grabbed one of his arms. "I can't believe it! It's finally time to go!"

Ted shook hands with his father and Uncle Enoch. He let his mother kiss his cheek without even making a face. He didn't care to have her kiss him in public, but he knew she was going to whether he liked it or not.

He and the Allertons went through the gates and into the train house. His uncle Daniel handed their tickets to a porter, who told them where to find their seats.

Ted's heart raced as he entered the car. Since his father was an engineer, he'd been on many trains. He'd even taken short train trips, sometimes riding in the engine with his father. But he'd never ridden in a fancy Pullman car with its velvet-covered seats and beds that folded down from the walls.

He and Esther shared a seat. Across the aisle, Richard and Anna took a seat that faced their parents.

"It's as pretty as a parlor in here," Esther said. "I didn't know there would be carpeting on the floors or wood paneling on the walls. And the seats are as comfortable as a chair at home."

Ted knew his uncle Daniel had paid more money so they could ride in the comfortable car. Passengers in other cars would be sitting up all night on hard seats.

The porter made a last call for passengers. Finally the car doors were closed, and the train chugged out of the huge train house. Ted and Esther watched as they rode past other trains, then past business houses.

Soon they were on the large, curving stone bridge that crossed the Mississippi River just above the Falls of St. Anthony. James Hill had built that bridge for his railroad, Ted remembered.

"Isn't it great to ride in one of Mr. Hill's trains across Mr. Hill's bridge?" Esther asked, her eyes shining.

Ted nodded.

"It was fun watching his parade," she went on.

Ted shifted uncomfortably on his seat. "Seattle planned a big parade and celebration for him, too. It was supposed to be held a month after the St. Paul parade."

Her green-eyed gaze darted to his face. "Supposed to be? What happened? Wasn't Seattle excited about the railroad?"

"The city had invited lots of important businessmen from across the country to take part in the celebration. Too many

49

businessmen were too broke to come because of the panic, so the city canceled it."

Esther heaved a sigh that lifted the shoulders of her new traveling outfit. "I'm glad we're going to the fair. I'm tired of hearing adults talk about money and bank runs."

"And bankrupt railroads," Ted continued her list, "and stock market trouble."

"I don't even know what a lot of the words mean," Esther said, "except that adults are afraid of losing their money and their jobs."

Ted nodded. "Seems all the adults are going about with long, worried faces and whispering about money problems."

"Fairs are fun places. At least there, no one should be sad and worried."

Ted hoped Esther was right. He tried to forget about James Hill and the country's money troubles. Instead he watched out the window with Esther as the train left the city and traveled along the river through countryside and small towns.

"I'm glad it's summer and the days are long," Esther said. "I want to see as much as I can before it gets dark."

"We'll be in Wisconsin before long," he told her. "We have to cross the entire state before we reach Illinois."

"How long will it take us to get there?"

"Let's see. We left at 5:15 this evening. We get there at 7:45 tomorrow morning. But it's really 6:45 our time. So I guess that's—"

"Thirteen and a half hours," Esther said promptly.

"Right. I read in the newspaper that it takes four days to get to Seattle from St. Paul."

"That must be an awfully long ways away, but I think it would be fun to go some day. Ted, why isn't the time in Chicago the same as in Minneapolis?"

"Because the railroads needed time they could count on."

Ted couldn't help feeling a bit proud that he knew something Esther didn't. "It used to be that towns could have whatever time they wanted. Wisconsin had thirty-eight different times."

"All for the same hour and minute?" Esther asked.

Ted nodded.

"That must have been confusing."

"The railroads needed to be able to tell what time it was easily, so the trains would arrive when people expected and to prevent accidents. But the whole country couldn't have the same time."

"Why?"

"Because the earth rotates. That means the sun rises earlier on the East Coast than on the West Coast. So the railroad people decided to have four different time zones in the United States to make travel easier. That was ten years ago."

"What time will it be in Seattle when we reach Chicago tomorrow morning?" Esther asked.

"Four forty-five."

Esther laughed. "That seems silly, but I guess it's no more silly than having thirty-eight times in one state for the same minute!"

After a couple hours, Ted grew tired of watching the small towns go past. He pulled his leather bag down from the brass bars above the seat and dug out a book.

"That's a good idea," Esther said. "I brought a book, too. I'm reading *David Copperfield*. What are you reading?"

"*Swiss Family Robinson.*" It was an exciting story, but Ted found himself looking out the window every few minutes, anyway. When twilight faded into night, he was amazed at how huge the sky looked and how bright the stars shone away from the city.

The conductor lighted lamps inside the car. It was time to get ready for bed. Porters pulled down sections of the walls and

51

made them into beds. The children used a tiny room at the back of the car to wash their faces and slip into their bed clothes.

Ted crawled into the berth above Esther's. He reached to shut the curtains that hid his bed from other people in the car.

"This is the most fun I ever had going to bed," Esther whispered as she closed her own curtains.

Ted didn't think he'd be able to sleep on the train, but he did. Soon, Aunt Marcia was waking him.

After using the small room to dress, wash, and comb his hair, he joined the others in the dining car for breakfast. Excitement spilled through him, though he tried not to show it. In just a couple hours, they'd be in Chicago!

CHAPTER 7

At the Fair

"Wow! The fair is as big as a town!" Ted peered out the window of the cigar-shaped car.

"This was a good idea you had, Ted," his uncle Daniel said from the seat across the aisle. "This train is built high enough so we can see all the buildings. It goes around the entire fairground. We'll be able to decide what to see first when we're done."

Ted grinned. "I wish Father could see this train. A train that travels on runners over water instead of on wheels over railroad tracks!"

Esther turned from the window. "Do you remember the Pledge of Allegiance, Ted?"

Ted nodded. Together they put their hands over their hearts and repeated: "I pledge allegiance to my flag and the Republic for which it stands; one nation, indivisible, with liberty and justice for all."

Aunt Marcia's eyebrows met in curiosity. "What is that verse?"

"It's the Pledge of Allegiance, Mother," Esther told her eagerly. "Our teacher taught it to us. She said that the day the World's Fair was dedicated last October, all the school children in the United States were going to say that pledge. That way, all of us had part in the World's Fair, even those children who don't get to come, like we do."

"Now we say it every day," Ted told her.

The train started, and the children immediately forgot about the pledge. They were too busy pointing out all the wonders they saw from the window—including Lake Michigan.

"Are you certain it's a lake?" Aunt Marcia teased. "It looks more like an ocean. I've never been to a lake where I couldn't see the opposite shore!"

After the train had been around the entire fair, Ted said, "Let's go to the Transportation Building first. I promised Father I'd go. It's right by one of the train stations, so we wouldn't have to walk far."

Everyone agreed. "Though I don't know what could be displayed in the Transportation Building that could be more exciting or newer than this water train," Uncle Daniel told Ted.

Richard was studying a large paper. "This says the building covers eighteen acres."

"Oh, my!" Anna looked down at her shoes with their pointed toes and groaned. "We're just starting, and my feet are already tired at the thought of all that walking."

Inside the huge building, the group went from exhibit to exhibit. One showed how railroad steam engines had been invented in the early 1800s and had changed over the years.

"Look at this train," Esther called to the others. "The cars look like stagecoaches!"

Richard pointed to the engine. "The engineer is standing at the back of the engine, and there isn't any cab. Your father wouldn't like that during a snowstorm, Ted!"

"He sure wouldn't," Ted agreed. He read a sign by the display. " 'This is a replica of the first railroad train in America, 1831, on Hudson and Mohawk line from Albany, New York, to Utica, New York.' Wow!"

"Wow!" Ted said again a few exhibits further. "New York Central's Engine No. 999!"

Esther gave a puzzled frown. "What's so special about it?"

Ted gaped at her. "What's so special? It only goes one hundred miles an hour!"

"Nothing goes one hundred miles an hour, Theodore Fisk!"

"This does," her father said, reading the signs beside the huge engine.

Ted leaned against the brass railing that kept the engine and visitors apart. "I wish I could touch it. Look at all that polished steel. It sure looks modern."

Esther tipped her head to one side, her brown curls spilling over her shoulder. "I like the colorful, painted engines like we see in Minneapolis better."

"Not me." Ted shook his head. "I think it's exciting to see things that are new."

Trains filled most of the Transportation Building—old trains and new ones. Ted and the Allertons saw most of them, and it took most of their morning to do so.

After the last train, Anna sat down on a step and rubbed her ankle. "I wish we could ride one of these trains through the building!"

Ted thought the last exhibit was the strangest. "An automobile. It only carries a couple people. Why would anyone need one of these when they could hire a carriage?"

Uncle Daniel shook his head. "I think this will be nothing but a toy for rich people."

Ted nodded solemnly.

"Let's visit the Agricultural Building next," Uncle Daniel suggested as they left the Transportation Building.

Esther groaned. "Must we, Father? Farming exhibits don't sound like much fun."

"Farming is important in Minnesota," her father said. "We need to see what Minnesota is telling the world about it."

"First, let's find something to eat," Aunt Marcia said, "or we won't have strength to see any more exhibits."

There was a restaurant right on the way to the Agricultural Building. Ted had never been so glad to see food!

When he was done eating, Richard studied his map of the fair. "The Agricultural Building is built on the Grand Basin. The view of the basin is supposed to be beautiful." He was right. When the basin came into view, they all stopped dead in their tracks.

"The White City," Aunt Marcia said in a low voice filled with wonder.

Esther seemed to be trying to see everything at once.

"Did they really build all these buildings just for the fair?"

"Yes," Richard told her, "and all the fair buildings that aren't on the basin, too."

The basin was about a third of a mile long. The buildings along it were covered with fake white rock and marble. The noon sunshine glistened off the buildings, making them shine.

Huge white pillars stretched across the opposite end of the basin. In the middle of them was an opening where small boats could float out into the harbor of Lake Michigan.

But right in front of them was Ted's favorite place on the basin: the Columbian Fountain, the largest fountain he'd ever seen. In the middle was a barge with four oarsmen on each side and a man operating a rudder in the rear. In the front was an angel-like creature with a trumpet. All around them were smaller statues of people and horses.

Ted leaned close to Esther and whispered, "I'd sure like to wade out in that fountain and climb up on one of those horses!"

Esther's face lit up with mischief. "Wouldn't that be fun? It would feel good, too. The sun is hot."

They didn't stay in the sunshine long. The Agricultural Building faced the basin and was almost as long as the basin itself. Soon they were inside.

Threshers, mowing machines, and other important farm machinery filled the bottom floor. Ted and Esther soon tired of them and went upstairs.

"I wish we could see something more exciting than this old Ag Building," Ted grumbled.

Esther yanked on his sleeve and pointed. "Look! It's the big flour mill from Minneapolis!"

Sure enough, there was a complete model of the Washburn-Crosby flour mill. Small flour barrels formed a barrier between visitors and the model. Ted and Esther went right up to the barrels so they could see as much as possible.

"It's just like the real thing." Esther's voice was filled with excitement. "All the company's mills and elevators are here."

"And their warehouses," Ted added, "and even the railroad tracks that run by the mills to carry grain to them and flour away when the grain is milled."

"Just think. Everyone who comes to the fair from everywhere else in the country—from all over the world, even—will see a piece of our own city."

Ted lifted his nose and sniffed. "It smells like fresh baked bread."

They followed their noses to the next exhibit. A mill made

flour while visitors watched. Beside it, women in dresses covered with neat white aprons made bread. Ted's mouth watered at the golden loaves they pulled from the ovens. When visitors were offered samples, he and Esther eagerly accepted. It seemed hours since they'd had lunch.

A boy about their own age, with curly blond hair and a round chin, stood beside Ted. He helped himself to a sample, too. Ted noticed the boy carried his threadbare jacket over his arm.

Ted and Esther ambled along the aisle. A man passed them wearing a jacket heavy with braid and a tiny hat with a strap under his chin.

"He looks like he's wearing a band uniform," Esther said with a laugh.

"He's one of the Columbian Guard," Ted explained. "That's what they call the fair police."

"Hey, lemme go!"

At the yell, they whirled around. The boy they'd seen a couple minutes ago was yelling. The policeman had one of the boy's arms in a tight grip. In the other, the policeman held a camera.

"No pictures allowed," the policeman said firmly. "That's the rule."

"Lemme go!" the boy yelled again. The policeman dragged him, kicking and screaming, down the aisle past Ted and Esther. "I ain't hurtin' nothin'!"

Why was the boy being arrested? Ted wondered. He'd only tried to take a picture of the miniature mill. Ted tried to forget the incident as he and Esther continued down the aisle.

A young woman at another exhibit was handing out samples. "Would you like to try our cereal?" she asked the cousins.

Ted frowned. "I thought cereal was oatmeal."

"This is a new kind of cereal," the woman told him. "It's called Shredded Wheat."

Esther looked into the small bowl the woman held out to them and made a face. "It looks like straw."

"Taste it," the woman urged.

Esther shook her head back and forth so quickly her curls flew beneath her straw sailor hat.

"You aren't going to be a chicken, are you?" asked a tall young man beside them.

Ted reached out slowly and took a small piece.

"How is it?" Esther asked.

"Not bad. It's crunchy."

"With milk, it turns soft," the woman told them. "And sugar makes it sweeter, just as it does oatmeal. This cereal will save housewives time because it doesn't need to be cooked."

Esther grinned. "But it's not warm like oatmeal. I like warm cereal on a cold Minnesota morning."

"Then you would like our other new cereal, Cream of Wheat," the woman said. She spooned some into a small bowl from a pot on the stove behind her, added a little sugar, and handed it to Esther along with a spoon.

Esther hesitated.

"Chicken?" Ted asked, teasing.

Esther's chin shot up. "I guess if you could try something, I can, too." She spooned a tiny bit of the creamy white mixture and blew on the spoon to cool it. Taking a deep breath, she popped the spoonful into her mouth and swallowed it quickly.

"Why, it's good!"

Ted and the woman laughed at her surprise.

But their favorite new food was a few exhibits away: a new sweet called Juicy Fruit Gum.

"Too bad we can't have this for breakfast!" Ted said to Esther as they walked away, chewing it.

A minute later, Esther's family joined them. Ted and Esther told them about the boy who had been arrested.

"There are only a couple men who can take pictures at the fair," Uncle Daniel explained. "They paid a fee for the right. If people want pictures, they have to buy them from those men. Even newspapers and magazines can't take pictures. That's why the boy was arrested."

"I guess I understand," Ted said slowly, "but it doesn't seem fair. The boy was only our age."

"We've seen enough for one day," Uncle Daniel said. "It's almost dinnertime. Let's catch a beach cart back to the hotel."

Disappointment swamped Ted. There was still so much to see!

But when they walked out onto the boardwalk that separated the fair from Lake Michigan, he forgot to be disappointed. Here was a magnificent lake that put the ten thousand lakes of Minnesota to shame. The cool breeze off the lake felt good after the hot summer sun that had beat down on the concrete walks.

In an inlet, three wooden ships bobbed. They looked very old, but small. "What are those ships?" Esther asked.

Richard knew the answer. "They are copies of the three ships Columbus brought over in 1492: the *Santa Maria,* the *Nina,* and the *Pinta.* They were built in Spain."

"I wouldn't want to cross the ocean in these ships," Ted said. "They're small!"

Ted remembered that the real name of this World's Fair was "The Columbian Exhibition." The fair had been dedicated in the fall of 1892, even though the buildings didn't open until the next spring. It was named after Columbus, who had reached America four hundred years earlier.

"I guess that boy should have taken pictures of Lake Michigan instead of the mill," Esther said to Ted in a sad voice. Ted nodded.

CHAPTER 8

Mr. Edison Arrives

"Be sure to act like a young lady today," Mother admonished Esther the next morning as they entered the fairgrounds.

Esther rolled her eyes. "No one here knows us, so I don't see why it matters how I act."

"Many important people from all over the world are visiting the fair," Father reminded her. "You never know when one of them might be standing beside you."

"Yes, Father," Esther said quietly.

He's right, Ted thought, remembering some of the important fair visitors they'd read about in the newspapers. Even a princess from Spain had come.

"Electricity Hall is the first place we'll visit today," Uncle Daniel said.

"Hurrah!" Ted grinned. "There's lots I want to see there."

Electricity Hall was much lighter than the buildings they'd visited the day before. The electric lights at the exhibits, along with the huge windows and the skylights, made the building bright.

In the middle of the downstairs display area, General Electric had built the Tower of Light, designed by Thomas Edison. Pillars taller than people surrounded the tower's base. The tower was covered with five thousand lightbulbs, blinking on and off. On top of the tower was an eight-foot model lightbulb, made of tiny prisms that reflected the light and made the light seem even brighter than it was.

"Have you ever seen so many lightbulbs?" Aunt Marcia asked, staring up at the tower, which reached almost to the ceiling.

"Mercy!" Anna shielded her eyes. "It's so bright I can barely look at it!"

"The tower is seventy feet high," Richard said. It seemed to Ted that Richard knew more facts about the fair than the rest of them put together.

"Oh!" Esther pointed past the nearby exhibits. "Look, Ted! That must be the Egyptian Temple!" She darted up the wide aisle toward the temple.

"Esther Marie Allerton!" Mother's voice was sharp with anger, but not loud enough for Esther to hear. Esther was already halfway to the temple.

Ted knew Aunt Marcia was too much of a lady to yell at

Esther in public. It wasn't considered proper.

"I'll catch her, Aunt Marcia," he said, "and remind her not to run." He walked as fast as he could.

Esther was standing in the doorway, looking at the strange hieroglyphics that bordered the doorway. Of course, it wasn't a real temple, but it was interesting.

Ted especially liked the pillars inside the temple. They glowed with green light. The only other light came from the window displays.

Esther shivered. "Those lights make the room look strange —kind of. . .eerie."

Ted thought so, too, but he still liked them.

When the rest of their group joined them, Aunt Marcia and Anna weren't nearly as impressed. "I think it's creepy," Anna said and walked away.

Her mother agreed. "I much prefer the cheerful displays."

"Are you ready to go upstairs?" asked Uncle Daniel.

Ted was filled with wonder at the things he saw upstairs. A door opened when he walked on a certain part of the floor. A person could write something down, and the writing would be sent to another part of the country by a new machine called a tel-auto-graph. In a walnut shell sat the world's smallest steam engine, which they looked at through a magnifying glass.

"Whatever are these chickens doing here?" Aunt Marcia asked, looking into a sandy enclosure.

Ted and Esther hurried to her side. "Oh, they're so cute!" Esther said, looking at the fluffy yellow chicks.

A small house made of curtains stood in the middle of the sand. Ted read the banner stretched across the house. " 'Who needs mother now!' "

"Well!" Aunt Marcia pretended to be insulted.

"What do chickens have to do with electricity?" Anna asked. "And why don't the chicks need a mother?"

A mustached young man attending the booth smiled at her. "If you'll step to the other side of the exhibit, you will see."

Ted and the Allertons did as he suggested. "This is called an incubator," the young man told them. "Electricity supplies the warmth needed to hatch the eggs and to keep the chicks warm. So as you can see, they don't need a mother."

Ted and the others stared through the side of the incubator. "Look! There's one hatching now!"

They watched, fascinated, while a little beak poked its way through a shell. In another part of the incubator, another chick broke free of the last of its shell.

"Poor thing," Esther exclaimed. "It looks cold and wet."

"It won't be for long," Ted said. "It's already headed for the lightbulb."

The damp chick stumbled and hopped to a lightbulb and leaned against it, gathering warmth.

"What do you do with the chicks?" Esther asked the man.

A smile beamed from beneath his mustache. "We give them away. Would you like one? I can put one in a box for you."

Esther swung around to her father. "May I? They are so sweet, and it would be such fun to watch one grow up."

Father laughed. "Where would you keep it while we visit the fair? It needs water and food and warmth."

"I could keep the box in our hotel room while we're at the fair," she suggested eagerly.

Richard shook his head. "I doubt the conductor of the Pullman car would let you keep the chick with you on the train. Besides, where would you keep a chicken at home?"

Esther turned to her mother.

Her mother lifted a finger. "Don't even ask, Esther Marie. I'll not have a chicken in my home or in my yard."

Ted flung an arm around his cousin's shoulders. "Don't

worry. I'm sure there are lots of children in Chicago who will give the chicks homes."

"At least until the chicks grow big enough to eat," Richard said cheerfully.

"Murderer!" Esther gave him a dark look.

Esther seemed to forget about the chicks when they entered the model home where everything was done by electricity. They entered after ringing an electric doorbell. Aunt Marcia smiled. "How charming!"

The home was filled with electric wonders: a fire alarm, hot plates, an electric iron, an electric sewing machine, an electric fan, an electric stove, a carpet sweeper, and even a washing machine.

"I want a home like this when I grow up," Esther declared.

"I want a home like this *now*," her mother added.

Uncle Daniel laughed and pulled her arm through his. "With all these inventions, there won't be anything left for a woman to do around the house."

"That suits me fine," Aunt Marcia declared.

"Me, too!" Esther and Anna chimed in.

Uncle Daniel's chuckle died away as he stood at the railing and looked down at the first floor. Ted stood beside him. Electrical wonders met his gaze everywhere he looked.

"This is a great time to be a child," his uncle said. "When I look at all these inventions, I get excited wondering what new things will be invented in your lifetimes."

"I wonder how many of these things were developed by Thomas Edison," Richard mused. "I read that it would take twenty-five acres just to display all the machines he's worked on."

"The things he's created have already changed the way people live," Uncle Daniel told them. "People say his creations will change the way people live in the twentieth century, too."

"He has a new invention here that I want to see," Richard said.

"His dynamo?" his father asked. "I understand he has one here. So do other inventors. Scientists say this kind of power will begin a new phase in history."

Richard shook his head. "What I want to see is much smaller than a dynamo."

His father swung out an arm. "Lead on."

As they were following Richard, Ted said, "I read in the newspaper that one hundred years from now, the person who is alive today who will be most remembered is Thomas Edison. Even more remembered than James Hill, the railroad king."

Esther grabbed Ted's sleeve so hard that she almost jerked him off balance. He heard her gasp.

"What is it?" he asked, tugging at his jacket sleeve and frowning.

She pointed toward three men in suits and bowler hats standing near the display they were passing. The men seemed to be in a friendly argument. They talked fast, laughed through their beards and mustaches, and waved their hands about as though trying to draw pictures in the air for each other.

"Isn't that. . .isn't it. . . Ed. . .Ed. . ."

"Edison. It's Thomas Edison," her father finished for her. His voice was low but filled with excitement.

Ted's heart seemed to jump to his throat and beat wildly.

Aunt Marcia laid her gloved hand on Uncle Daniel's forearm. "Are you sure it's Mr. Edison?"

"Oh, yes, I'm sure," he answered. "I've seen his picture in newspapers and magazines often enough."

"Me, too," Richard agreed. "I sure wish we had a camera!"

Esther looked up at her father. "Can we meet him, Father? We could introduce ourselves."

"I'm afraid not." Uncle Daniel shook his head, but Ted

66

thought he looked like he wanted to say yes. "It wouldn't be polite. If he were meeting strangers, there would be others about him."

"But maybe those men he's talking to were strangers, too," Esther pressed.

Her mother smiled. "I doubt that. They appear to know each other well."

She laid a gentle hand on Richard's arm. "Let us move on to the exhibit you wanted to show us. It isn't polite to gawk at people, even if they are famous."

They moved on slowly. In spite of Aunt Marcia's words, Ted couldn't help watching the great man. He noticed Esther was doing the same. She walked as close as she could to the three men as they passed. Ted stayed right beside her.

"I've heard that you believe in a personal God," one of the men was saying to Edison. "Is that true?"

"Certainly," the white-haired genius nodded. "The existence of a God can almost be proven by chemistry. Look at the atoms, at the orderly way the universe is put together. Could this have happened without a great, intelligent God?"

Ted and Esther smiled at each other. Once they were out of earshot, they kept on craning their necks to watch the famous man. Ted twisted his head about until his neck hurt. Suddenly he bumped into Esther.

Aunt Marcia cried out, falling against Uncle Daniel.

Ted saw in a flash that Esther had bumped into her mother before he had bumped into Esther.

Uncle Daniel caught Aunt Marcia before she could fall but not before her pride was hurt. Her cheeks flamed dark red. Ted groaned, and he saw Esther squeeze her eyes shut and wince.

"I'm sorry, Mother." Esther's apology rushed out. "I was watching. . .that is. . ."

Ted knew she'd remembered just in time that they weren't

supposed to be gawking at Mr. Edison.

Aunt Marcia straightened her new hat. "You were ogling Mr. Edison, weren't you?"

For a minute Ted thought Esther was going to deny it. Then she clasped her hands behind her new green dress, looked at the floor, and nodded.

Aunt Marcia sighed deeply. "I can hardly blame you, though it *was* rude. It was also dangerous. What if I had been a stranger without a husband to catch me from falling? You could have hurt someone."

"Yes, ma'am," Esther murmured. "I'll try to be more careful, I promise."

Richard interrupted. "This is the exhibit I wanted to see. It's Edison's new kinetoscope."

"His what?" Ted asked.

"Kinetoscope," Richard answered. "You look into a box at picture film. There's a magnifying glass, and the film has an electric light behind it so you can see the picture."

"Like a stereoscope with a light?" Aunt Marcia asked.

"What is new about looking at pictures?" Esther demanded.

"Don't you read anything in the newspapers?" Richard asked. "These pictures move."

"*Moving* pictures?" Ted grinned. "You're pulling our legs."

Richard didn't smile. "Not only do the pictures move, but they talk."

Ted laughed again.

"You'll see." Richard turned on his heel and entered the exhibit.

Ted and the others followed. Inside was a box about two feet square. It stood four feet high. Beside it stood a phonograph.

Richard climbed up on a stool. The man in charge of the booth handed him earphones. Then Richard looked down into the box. "Wow!"

Ted thought he sounded almost as excited as Uncle Daniel had when they saw Edison.

In less than a minute, Richard was removing the headphones and climbing down from the stool. A grin spread from ear to ear. His black eyes shone like new marbles. "That's fantastic!"

Ted waited impatiently to see what was so fantastic. All the Allertons climbed the stool and looked into the box first. Each one came away looking as excited as Richard had.

Esther was the last of the Allertons to view it. "You won't believe it, Ted!"

He climbed the stool eagerly and fitted the earphones over his head. He looked through a small slit on top of the box.

He saw a picture of a blacksmith. The blacksmith began moving! Ted gasped. The blacksmith used his sledgehammer and tongs, then laughed and looked like he was talking to friends in his blacksmith shop. The film stopped.

Ted was disappointed and excited at the same time. "That was great! I wish it would have lasted longer, though. Do you think Mr. Edison will sell his kinetoscopes for people to use in their homes with their phonographs, Uncle Daniel?"

His uncle grinned. "I expect they will be toys for rich people, like the automobiles we saw in the Transportation Building yesterday."

Ted spread his arms wide and laughed. "Well, I guess I'm just going to have to get rich one day! Now all I have to do is figure out how!"

When they left the booth, Ted glanced down the aisle, hoping for another glimpse of Mr. Edison. He was still there, but so was a small crowd. A man in a suit was angrily trying to grab a black box from one of the fair's policemen.

"What's happening?" Ted asked the guide who was standing outside the booth they'd just left.

The man nodded toward the disturbance. "A newspaper

reporter tried to take a picture of Mr. Edison. The policeman took away his camera."

Ted felt like he'd swallowed a rock. The scene reminded him of the boy he and Esther had seen arrested the day before. He glanced at Esther. Her face looked as sad as he felt.

"Don't gawk," Anna reminded them.

Ted bit back an angry retort. Fourteen-year-old Anna sounded just like her mother.

Uncle Daniel cleared his throat. "Let's find a restaurant and have lunch. Then how about a ride on the Ferris wheel?"

Excitement sent a chill through Ted. Esther grabbed his arm and bounced up and down. They'd been able to see the Ferris wheel whenever they were outside. It was much taller than any of the buildings. Ted had never been up as high as it went. And in an hour or two, he'd be on it!

CHAPTER 9

Trouble on the Midway

As hungry as he'd been after spending all morning walking around Electricity Hall, Ted didn't think they'd ever get done eating and over to the Ferris wheel. Only Aunt Marcia's constant reminders kept him and Esther from running all the way from the restaurant to the wheel that towered over the fair.

Aunt Marcia raised her parasol to protect herself from the noonday sun. "I do wish we didn't have to go so far down the Midway to ride the Ferris wheel. I've heard the Midway is

71

filled with inappropriate displays."

Ted opened his mouth to say something, then shut it tight. He'd heard the Midway was filled with fun exhibits, but Esther's mother often seemed to think fun was "inappropriate." Ted's mother said it was because Aunt Marcia was a proper lady and that more women should act like her.

Anna opened her parasol and leaned it against her shoulder. Ted smiled. She was always copying her mother. No wonder Aunt Marcia thought Anna was a perfect young lady.

Esther wrinkled her brow. "How is the Midway different from the rest of the fair?" she asked Richard.

"The Midway is more like a circus than like the White City."

The wide Midway was even more crowded than the walkways by the White City. Women with parasols and men in bowler hats or smart round straw hats peered in wonder at the buildings and exhibits that edged the street.

Roar!

Ted jumped. "What was that?"

Richard laughed. "A lion. Behind those walls on our left is a big animal show. Can't you read the signs?"

Ted grinned sheepishly. He'd been so intent on the huge wheel at the end of the street that he wasn't paying attention to what they were passing.

He looked to the other side of the street. He wasn't going to be caught daydreaming again! "That looks like a castle. The sign on it says Blarney Castle."

"It's a copy of a castle in Ireland," Richard explained. "Ireland sent over the Blarney Stone, and it's here in Blarney Castle. Legend says that if you kiss the Blarney Stone, you will have a wonderful way with words all your life."

Soft music filled the air. "That doesn't sound Irish," Esther said.

They all stopped and watched young Japanese women

with gongs and tinkling bells. The music seemed almost too sweet for the busy street, Ted thought.

A few steps later a stronger beat caught his attention. South Sea Islanders sat above the opening for their exhibit. The dark men wore only small cloths around their hips. They pounded out music on hollow logs.

Ted barely noticed the German and Turkish villages they passed next. He was too intent on the Ferris wheel, which seemed to grow larger as they neared it.

When they reached the ticket line, Ted and the others stared up, up at the revolving wheel.

"Oh, my," Aunt Marcia said in a little voice. One gloved hand slipped to her lace-covered neck. "It's so big and so high. Are you sure it is safe?"

"Absolutely," answered Richard, who had his trusty guidebook in hand. "Thousands, maybe millions, of people have ridden it since the fair started."

"I suppose," his mother said in that same tiny voice.

Ted followed her gaze back into the sky. The monstrous wheel did make a person feel small, but that didn't frighten him. He glanced at Esther. From the way her eyes sparkled, he knew she was as excited as he was.

Richard studied his book. "It says here that the wheel was designed by George Washington Gale Ferris—that's why it's called the Ferris wheel."

"Even I could have guessed that," Esther said, giving him a withering look.

Ted hid a grin. Sometimes Richard did sound like a know-it-all, but he had to admit he liked finding out what Richard knew about the things they saw.

"He built the Ferris wheel for the fair," Richard continued. "The fair planners wanted something that would be as spectacular as the Eiffel Tower that was built for the Paris fair."

Uncle Daniel paid for their tickets, and Ted swallowed a cry of surprise. Fifty cents each! That was as much as it cost to get into the entire fair. He remembered his father saying the cost was way too much for a working man.

The unhappiness of the country's money troubles swept over him. He pushed it away, angry that it had intruded on this wonderful day of fun.

The Ferris wheel came to a stop. The door of a large car was opened, and people poured out. They chatted eagerly with each other about the sights they'd seen from the wheel.

Ted and the Allertons filed into the glass and wood car and sat down in the plush swivel seats. Ted counted the seats while other passengers filed in. "Forty seats! And the sign near the ticket window said there are thirty-six cars on the Ferris wheel."

"Each car can hold twenty standing passengers besides," Richard said.

"That means the Ferris wheel can carry over two thousand people at once!" Esther's voice was filled with awe.

"Oh, dear," Aunt Marcia said in her small voice. "Are you certain it won't fall down?"

Uncle Daniel patted her gloved hand and smiled down at her. "I promise it won't fall down, my dear."

The door closed, and the car began to move.

Ted and Esther shared excited glances. Then Ted looked out the glass windows that went from ceiling to floor all about the car.

The car rose many feet, then stopped. Ted looked down at the Midway. "The people look small from up here." Soon it started up once more.

When it stopped again, they were quite high above the buildings and could see a long way. The White City gleamed bright as ice cream in the sunshine. Its lagoons and basins were blue in the midst of the beautiful buildings.

"Oh, it's lovely!" Aunt Marcia leaned forward eagerly.

Ted and Esther grinned at each other. "Mother seems to have forgotten to be afraid," Esther whispered.

The next stop was at the very top of the Ferris wheel. "Wow! We're over two hundred fifty feet above the earth!" Richard said.

Ted's heart beat faster at the very thought. He almost expected Aunt Marcia to say "Oh, my" again, but she didn't. Instead she pointed beyond the White City to a huge expanse of blue that seemed to meet the sky. "There's our hotel and Lake Michigan."

"The lake looks like it goes on forever," Esther said. "I know there's a shore on the other side, but it's hard to believe when you see the lake like this."

"Yes, it is," Ted agreed. "You'd think from this high, a person could almost see the other end of the earth."

"Or at least to Minneapolis," Esther teased.

As the wheel started down the opposite side, the people in the car turned their swivel seats and looked down the Midway. The shadow of the great wheel filled the street for a long way.

"There's the German Village, and the Blarney Castle, and the animal show," Ted said.

"And there's the elevated railroad we rode on the first day." Richard pointed out the track that ran a block behind the Midway.

Ted laughed. "The railroad seemed high when we rode on it. From up here it looks like a toy train."

When the car reached the bottom, Aunt Marcia stood up. "Well, I must say, I am almost sorry our ride is over."

"It's not, dear," Uncle Daniel told her. "We get to go around one more time."

When they finally left the car, Esther looked up at her father. "May we go again? Please?"

"Not today," he answered. "Perhaps later in the week."

Ted would have liked to go again, too. *But at fifty cents a person, I wouldn't dare ask,* he thought. If it weren't for his uncle, he wouldn't have seen the fair at all or ridden in the Ferris wheel. "Thank you, Uncle Daniel. It was great!"

His uncle winked at him. "Glad you enjoyed it."

"I think I could use some refreshment," Aunt Marcia said, brushing the folds out of the skirt of her navy blue walking suit. "Let's stop for something to drink and maybe a sweet."

"I'd rather visit some more exhibits, Mother," Richard said hesitantly.

"Me, too!" Esther chimed in.

"I'm not hungry yet, Mother," Anna added. "We did eat right before we went on the Ferris wheel."

"May we visit some of the exhibits while you and Father relax?" Richard asked.

Aunt Marcia frowned slightly and glanced at her husband. "I'm not sure that's a good idea."

"We'll be careful," Richard assured her.

"I'm sure they will be fine," Uncle Daniel told her. "Richard and Anna are responsible."

Aunt Marcia's frown still wrinkled her forehead. "Will you watch out for Ted and Esther?" she asked Richard and Anna.

They nodded.

Esther groaned. "We can watch out for ourselves. We are twelve years old."

Aunt Marcia looked firmly at Esther. "See that you mind Richard and Anna. And behave like a young lady."

Esther rolled her eyes but agreed.

"You'll need some money if you want to go inside some of the exhibits." Uncle Daniel handed Richard some money.

"Don't spend any of it on the inappropriate places," Aunt Marcia warned.

"No, Mother, we won't," Richard promised.

"Be back here in an hour," Aunt Marcia instructed.

"But that's hardly any time!" Esther cried.

"She's right, Mother," Richard said. "Can't we meet you back here at, say, five o'clock?"

The Allertons looked at each other. Ted held his breath, hoping they'd say yes.

They did, and the children hurried down the street.

"Watch out! Watch o-o-out!"

Ted leaped back. A boy who looked to be about ten led a swaying smelly camel past him. On top of the camel a young woman clutched a rope with one hand and her hat with the other. She rocked forward, then jerked back at the camel's next step.

"Camel rides! That looks like fun," Ted called to Richard.

"Watch out!"

Ted looked to his left, expecting to see another camel. This time it was a donkey being led by a boy. The legs of the young man riding the donkey almost hit the ground.

"They're from the Street in Cairo exhibit," Richard said.

"Let's each ride one!" Esther suggested.

"You won't catch me on one of those smelly beasts," Anna declared. "I want to go where we can get out of the sun. Let's visit the Viennese Buildings, Richard."

Ted looked longingly over his shoulder at Cairo Street but followed the others toward the entrance toward Old Vienna. "It costs twenty-five cents each to get in here." Ted pointed to the sign above the arched gateway. He hoped Richard would rather go back to Cairo Street than pay a dollar for all of them to visit Old Vienna. Richard only smiled and bought the tickets.

The street looked like a place in Old Vienna in 1750. Ted thought it was mildly interesting, but Richard and Anna thought it was wonderful.

Ted enjoyed the portraits of Egyptian mummy cases better. "Never know what you're going to see at the fair, do you?" he asked Esther.

"I wish Richard and Anna didn't take so long to see everything, though," she whispered.

Ted nodded.

Esther cleared her throat. "Richard, Ted and I are tired. We want to go out and find something to drink."

Anna frowned. "We aren't done looking here yet."

Esther ignored her. "We won't get into any trouble, Richard."

"Well," Richard hesitated. He glanced at Anna, then at Ted and Esther. "I suppose, if you're sure to meet us in front of here."

"We promise," Esther said over her shoulder as she and Ted hurried away.

Esther took a deep breath when they were back on the Midway. "I'm sure glad to be out of there! Let's try to find where we can ride the camels."

They hurried through the crowded street, dodging men's elbows, women's parasols, and an occasional tall-backed wheeled chair. "Anna and Mother should rent wheeled chairs," Esther told Ted. "They're always complaining their feet are hurting."

Ted stopped a boy leading a donkey with a laughing five-year-old girl on top of it. "Where are the camel rides?"

"On Cairo Street." The boy pointed toward the Ferris wheel.

"I wish adults didn't always walk so slow!" Esther grumbled. She darted around two men and a woman who were walking together.

Ted heard a crash and yells. A moment later he saw Esther in the middle of a tumble of people and a wheeled chair.

"Oh, no!"

The chair lay on its side. One large back wheel spun madly. An elderly lady in an expensive-looking purple dress was caught in the tipped-over chair beneath a sprawled Esther.

CHAPTER 10
The Mysterious Boy

"Why don't you watch where you're going?" The college-aged chair boy grabbed Esther by one arm and yanked her up.

"Ouch!" Esther clutched her shoulder. Running into the chair had knocked the breath out of her, but it hadn't hurt. The way the boy had pulled her up made her arm feel like it was on fire.

Ted rushed up to Esther. "Are you hurt?"

She shook her head and made herself quit holding her shoulder. "No."

The chair boy was already kneeling beside the woman. Esther knelt beside the chair, too. She put a hand on the woman's arm. "Are you hurt?"

"I. . .I don't think so," the woman said. "Do you always

dart about in such an unladylike manner?"

Esther winced. "I'm afraid I do."

Esther tried to ignore the pain in her shoulder as she and the chair boy helped the woman to her feet. While the chair boy righted the large, heavy chair, she turned to look for the woman's hat and for her own.

"Oh, no!" she whispered when she saw them.

Her own little sailor hat with its broad navy blue satin ribbon was squashed flat where some passerby had stepped on it. She watched Ted pick it up and give her a pitying glance.

Worse was the lady's hat. A boy about her own age had sat on it! He was busy dusting the dirt from his frayed knickers, not paying any attention to the bonnet he'd ruined. The curly-haired boy looked familiar, but she was sure she didn't know him.

She picked up the bonnet. It had been a perfectly delightful little hat, she could tell. A deep purple ribbon sat over the point in front. White silk roses peeked from behind it. At the back was another glossy purple bow.

She turned back to the woman, who the chair boy was helping back into the chair. Swallowing hard, she handed the hat to the woman. "I'm terribly sorry, ma'am; just terribly."

"Well, that doesn't restore my bonnet, does it?" The woman set her lips in a hard line.

"N. . .no, ma'am." Esther rubbed her suddenly sweaty hands down the sides of her skirt. "I. . .I guess I should offer to pay for it."

"That's the least you can do!" the chair boy agreed in a nasty tone.

Esther's gaze darted to his angry blue eyes and back to the woman. "I truly am sorry. I only have about twenty-five cents with me today. If you will tell me how much the bonnet cost and give me your address, I'll send you the money."

The hard lips relaxed a little. The woman waved a black-gloved hand. "Oh, never mind. I'm sure you didn't intend to run me down."

"I. . .thank you, ma'am," Esther whispered. "Are you sure you weren't hurt?"

"Only a couple bumps and bruises." She actually smiled. "This old body has known worse. I do remember being young and how it felt to run about on a summer's day. But you must be more careful."

"Yes, ma'am."

The chair boy scowled at Esther as he leaned into the back of the chair and started it again. The woman waved good-bye, and Esther lifted a hand in farewell. She wanted to stick her tongue out at the chair boy, but even she was too ladylike to do that!

"Is Mother ever going to be mad when she sees my hat," she said, turning back to Ted. "It seems I'm never able to hide my accidents from her."

"Ya mean yer like this all the time?" The boy who had sat on the lady's hat scowled from beneath curly blond hair. "Why don't ya watch where yer goin'? Think yer the only person in the street?"

Esther's cheeks grew hot at his angry words. "I didn't tip over the chair on purpose. And you're the one who sat on the lady's hat."

"Esther." Ted's voice held a warning tone. She looked at him. "When you knocked over the chair, you knocked him over, too. He was walking on the other side of it."

Esther stared at the boy's scowling face. "Oh." She cleared her throat. "I mean, I'm sorry."

"Ya should be sorry. Why don't ya act like a lady?" He hit his flat-topped hat against the side of his knickers before stuffing it over his curls.

Esther's green eyes blazed. "Why, you. . .you. . .how dare you say that to me."

He held out a hand, palm up. "Ya can give me that twenty-five cents yer carryin', too."

"I'm not going to give—"

"Ya wrecked my doughnuts."

"Your doughnuts?"

"His doughnuts," Ted repeated.

She glanced at him. His arms were full of golden doughnuts. "I think he was selling them," Ted said.

"That's right." The boy crossed his arms over his chest. A cloth bag hung from one shoulder. Esther could see it looked lumpy and decided that must be where he was carrying the rest of the doughnuts.

"I'm sorry I ruined your doughnuts," she said, "but surely they aren't worth twenty-five whole cents."

"A chap's gotta make a livin'." He held out his hand again.

Esther reached for her pocketbook and drew out her precious quarter. She'd been hoping to buy a camel ride with it. Reluctantly she placed it in his hand.

He dropped it into his knickers' pocket without a word.

"You haven't very good manners," she scolded. "You might at least have said thank you."

A sneer curled his lip. "Thank ya fer ruinin' my doughnuts, miss."

"Oh!" She curled her hands into fists at her side and stamped her foot. She knew she should be sorry for knocking him down and ruining his doughnuts, but he was such a nasty boy that she didn't feel sorry at all.

Something about him looked familiar. "Don't I know you?" She frowned. "Why, you're the boy who was arrested for taking pictures of the flour mill!"

"That's where I've seen you!" Ted cried out.

The boy's round chin jerked up. His blue eyes flashed. "What's it to ya?"

Esther could hardly believe she'd felt sorry for this boy yesterday.

Ted must not have felt any of her frustration, for he said, "We thought it was terrible that you were arrested like that for taking pictures. Hadn't you heard that people aren't allowed to take pictures at the fair?"

"Yeah, I heard." Anger filled the boy's voice. "But a feller has ta make a livin'."

Esther remembered how this boy had reminded her of the newsboy, Erik, yesterday. Her anger began to go away. "Is. . . is your father dead?"

The round chin lifted even higher. Esther thought if he were any taller, he'd be looking down his wide nose at her. "No, Pa's not dead. He's just out of a job, like most of Chicago."

That's why he'd reminded her of Erik. Both their fathers were out of work, and both of them were filled with anger and sadness.

"I'm sorry," she said.

The boy's eyes flashed. "I don't need yer pity."

"We have a friend whose father is out of work," Ted said. "Our friend had to go to work, too." He held out his hand. "My name is Ted, and this is my cousin Esther. We're from Minneapolis."

The boy's blue-eyed gaze looked at Ted warily for a few minutes. Finally he shook Ted's hand. "I'm Frank Wells."

"Can I buy a good doughnut from you?" Ted asked. "I'm pretty hungry."

Frank dug into his bag and pulled out a golden brown doughnut. Esther's mouth watered. She wished she had some money left to buy one.

"They're a penny each," Frank said.

84

Ted dug a small leather pouch from his knickers' pocket and pulled out a penny. Breaking the doughnut in half, he handed part to Esther.

"These are really good," she told Frank after the first bite.

"My ma made them."

"How did you get back into the fair after being arrested yesterday?" Ted asked.

Frank shrugged, but he looked proud of himself. "It wasn't hard. There's lots of entrances to the fair. There's 2,500 fair police. Only a couple of them know I was caught with the camera."

"Did they put you in jail?" Esther asked. She'd never known anyone who had been arrested before.

"Naw. The judge said since I was a kid, he wouldn't make me pay the forty-dollar fine for bringing a camera into the fair, either."

"Did you get your camera back?" Ted asked.

"Yeah, but it belongs to a friend's pa so I didn't think I better try smugglin' it in again." Frank shook his head. "Too bad, too. Make a lot more money sellin' pictures than sellin' doughnuts, even though the doughnuts sell pretty good. 'Course, doughnuts can get me thrown out of the fair, too."

Esther tilted her head to one side. "Why would anyone care if you sell doughnuts?"

"Ya can't sell anything at the fair unless ya buy a license. The license costs more money than I've got."

"Is it true most of the people in Chicago are unemployed like you said?" Esther asked Frank.

"Well, maybe it just seems like it," Frank admitted. "But the newspaper says about three hundred thousand men in Chicago don't have jobs."

Ted let out a low whistle.

Esther wished there was something she could do to help

Frank and Erik and their fathers. She hated the helpless feeling that filled her when she thought of their troubles.

"We were going to ride the camels," Ted told Frank, "but we don't have enough money left. Since you know the fair so well, what do you think we should see?"

A mischievous gleam shone from Frank's eyes. "Follow me."

The look on Frank's face made Esther wonder if they should go with him. But he had already started down the hot, busy Midway with Ted on his worn heels. If she didn't start right away, she might lose them in the crowd.

Carrying her broken hat, she hurried after them.

CHAPTER 11

Caught!

From each side of the street, men and women called to people, inviting them to visit the exhibits. The invitations came in many languages, many accents, and sometimes in broken English. Ted and Esther had to watch out for camels and donkeys and wheeled chairs. Venders offered all kinds of things for sale: jewelry, food, drinks, official photographs.

Frank hurried past the places as though they were as familiar to him as Esther's home street was to her. She would have liked to linger at some of the shops and more unusual exhibits but didn't dare let the boys get too far ahead.

"Magic! Come see the Houdini Brothers escape from handcuffs!" A big man in a brown-checked suit called to the passersby.

Esther started to cross the street when she noticed Ted and Frank stopping at the door beside the large man with the booming voice.

She hurried over to them and jerked Ted's sleeve. "We can't go in there."

Frank gave her a smug look. "Scared?"

She was a little scared of anything with the word *magic* beside it, but she didn't want this tough boy to know it. She brushed her curls back from her shoulders and jerked her chin up in the air. "Of course not. It's just not appropriate entertainment for a young lady."

Ted bit his bottom lip. Then he said to Frank, "She's right. Her mother would never let us see a magic show."

Frank looked up at the sky. He took a deep breath that lifted his chest beneath his thin, mended cotton shirt. "It's not *real* magic. It's all about trickin' people. Don'cha know anything? That's the fun of it, tryin' ta figure out how the guys do it." He leaned closer to them.

"These guys are really good," Frank said in a low voice, nodding as if to make sure they believed him.

"Well. . ." Ted looked at her with a question in his brown eyes. "It would be fun to see someone try to get out of handcuffs without a key."

Esther nodded. "Mother and Father shouldn't mind if it's not truly magic." She ignored the sliver of guilt that prickled at her conscience. Ted was right. It did sound like fun.

Ted had to pay ten cents for himself and Esther to go inside. Frank simply handed the ticket seller a doughnut. "Hiya, Jack. Can I go in and sell my doughnuts?"

"Sure, Frank," the skinny, bald man said. "Just see ya don't keep payin' stooges from watchin' the show, hear?"

Frank gave him a sharp nod and touched the brim of his flat-topped hat. "Sure, I hear ya. Thanks."

Inside it seemed dark after the bright, sunlit street. Esther stumbled behind the boys until they found some empty wooden chairs.

Frank said, "I'll be back. I'm goin' ta try and sell some doughnuts before the show starts." He walked up and down the aisles. "Doughnuts! Only a penny apiece!"

A couple minutes later a man came on the small stage and announced two young men: Harry and Dash Houdini.

Frank hurried back up the aisle. "That's them," he said in a loud whisper before sitting down beside Ted.

Two short men with wavy black hair walked onstage. They wore suits that Esther thought looked like the suits the waiters at the hotel restaurant wore.

"They don't look any older than Richard," she whispered to Ted, who nodded in agreement.

The older one flashed a big smile. "Ladies and Gents, we're here to show youse a few experiments in de art of sleight o' hand."

The two performers made scarves appear and disappear. They did card tricks. They weren't very good. The older-looking brother dropped the cards. He shrugged his shoulders and gave the audience a big boyish grin. Most of the people laughed.

"That's Harry Houdini," Frank whispered. "He's not very good at this kind of thing, but wait until they do their escape tricks."

Esther wondered if they had wasted Ted's money.

Then the younger brother, Dash, pointed to someone standing between the stage and the audience at the edge of the room. "Youse there, come on up here an help us wid this experiment."

One of the fair policemen walked up onstage.

Esther gasped. "Aren't you afraid he'll catch you selling doughnuts, Frank?"

Frank waved a hand impatiently. "Naw. That's Al. He's a

friend of mine. The Houdini Brothers pay him to be part of their act when he's not on duty as a policeman."

Harry Houdini rolled up the sleeves of his short black jacket and his white shirt. He held out his arms toward the audience. "Youse can see I ain't got nothin' up my sleeves."

He held his hands toward Al, his wrists together. "Put on yer bracelets."

Al snapped the cuffs on. Then he held the key high for the audience to see and stuffed it into his own pocket. Another volunteer was called up from the audience to make sure the handcuffs were tightly fastened.

Harry Houdini wiggled his hands about, trying to slip his wrists from the cuffs. His boyish face screwed into wrinkles as he struggled. Esther leaned forward in her seat, holding her breath.

Suddenly Houdini whipped the cuffs from his wrists and, grinning, held them above his head.

Esther and Ted pounded their hands together until they stung. The rest of the audience did the same. Frank stuck two fingers between his lips and whistled.

The curtain at the back of the stage opened, and a stage hand wheeled a large box forward. The box was taller than the Houdinis.

Dash Houdini swung an arm toward the box. "Ladies and Gents, the Metamorphosis!"

It took Esther a minute to remember that the long word meant change.

The Houdini Brothers opened the box, letting the audience see it was empty. Then they turned the box all the way around.

"As youse can see," Dash told them, "there's only one way outa this box." He held up a strip of braid, dangling it before the audience.

Harry Houdini held his hands behind his back, wrists

together once more. Dash tied the braid around them. At Dash's request, Al the policeman checked the ropes to be sure they were tied tightly.

Then Harry Houdini walked inside the box. Dash closed the door and locked it.

Esther gasped. So did Ted and the rest of the audience.

Dash wrapped a long rope around the box, hesitated, then wrapped it around again and tied it. Once more, Al checked the rope and declared it was securely tied.

Esther inched forward on her seat. Her fingers clutched the top of the wooden chair in front of her. Her gaze was glued to the stage.

The stage curtains closed, hiding the box and Dash Houdini.

Dash's head appeared through the curtain. "One, two. . ." His head disappeared.

"Three!" Harry's face poked through the curtains where Dash's face had been a moment before.

Esther clapped a hand to her mouth. "Oh!"

Ted whooped.

The curtains parted. There stood the box, the door open. The rope lay on the floor. Inside stood Dash, his hands tied behind his back with the braid, just as Harry Houdini's had been.

The room thundered with applause and cheers. With huge smiles on their faces, the Houdinis bowed.

"That was great!" Ted said.

"Didn't I tell ya?" Frank gave him a smug smile.

"You said it's all a trick," Esther reminded him. "How did they do it? And so quickly?"

Frank looked at her in a way that made her feel sure he thought she was stupid. "They aren't likely ta be tellin' folks that. If they did, no one would pay to see them do their tricks."

"What else should we see?" Ted asked, as they blinked their way into the outdoors.

A smile slipped across Frank's round face. "Come on. I'll introduce you to a friend of mine."

"Watch out! Watch out!"

Esther stepped out of the way as a camel passed with its passenger. *If I'd been watching where I was going, I could be riding one of them,* she thought, disgusted with herself.

Frank stopped in front of an exhibit. "This is it."

Cheerful piano music came from the exhibit, the notes pushing aside the sounds of the street. Curious, Esther and Ted followed Frank inside.

A young black man was playing the piano. His hands flew across the white and black keys.

Esther leaned close to Ted so he could hear her. "He looks like he's having a good time." She bounced up and down to the music.

Applause filled the room when the man finished. He stood up and bowed. "More!" cried someone in the audience. The rest of the audience clapped harder and repeated the cry.

The young man shook his head, smiling. "Time to give these fingers a break. I'll be back before long, though. Thanks for coming." He walked behind a curtain.

"He was good," Esther told Frank. "I'm glad you brought us here."

The crowd began filing out. Frank didn't follow. Instead he headed toward the stage.

Esther and Ted looked at each other uncertainly.

Frank turned around and motioned for them to follow him. When he disappeared behind the curtain, Esther looked at Ted again. He shrugged and followed Frank, so Esther slipped behind the curtain, too.

Frank greeted a couple of the men who were working behind stage. The black man who'd been playing the piano was standing at the back of the room, drinking a glass of water.

Esther stared as Frank walked right up to him. "Hi, Mr. Joplin."

"Frank! Good to see you again. I could use one of those doughnuts of your mother's, if you have any left. I'm famished."

Frank pulled one out of his bag and received a penny from Mr. Joplin.

"I brought some new friends by to hear your music," Frank told him.

Esther's heart swelled at the word 'friends.' *I hope that means he's forgiven me for ruining so many doughnuts,* she thought.

"This is Ted and Esther," Frank told the man. His shoulders seemed to straighten a bit in pride. "And this is Mr. Scott Joplin. He's about the best piano player that's ever lived."

Mr. Joplin laughed. "Wish everyone felt like you do, Frank."

"I liked your music," Esther said. "I don't think I've ever heard anything like it, though."

Mr. Joplin smiled at her. "I call it Ragtime."

"Why don't you play popular music," Ted asked, "like the bands and orchestras back home?"

"The world always needs new kinds of music, don't you think? Ragtime is the kind of music I hear in my head. When I sit down at a piano, it just seems to come out the tips of my fingers and make these ivories dance."

Esther grinned. "I wish I could do that. It must be fun to have cheerful music in your head and fingers."

Mr. Joplin winked at her. "Little lady, I like the way you think."

Esther thought Mr. Joplin's break went by all too fast. She'd enjoyed talking with him. "Can we listen to more of his music before we leave?" she asked Frank.

"Sure." He took a doughnut from his bag and munched it

93

while they waited for Mr. Joplin to be introduced.

Suddenly she heard Frank gasp. She swung her head toward him. A large hand was clamped onto one of Frank's shoulders. An angry face on top of a big man in a fair policeman's uniform glared down. "Caught up with you again, you little thief!"

CHAPTER 12
Frank's Escape

"I'm no thief!" Frank twisted his shoulders, but he couldn't break the policeman's hold.

The big man snorted. "By selling your wares without a license, you're stealing money from honest food vendors. If that's not being a thief, I don't know what is."

People in the audience stared, wondering about the ruckus. Frank's cheeks glowed bright red.

Esther glared at the man. Her hands balled into fists at her side. "You don't have to be so rough."

"Don't meddle in police business, little lady. Say!" The man squinted his beady eyes at her. "Are you with this robber?"

Esther opened her mouth to say yes, but Ted answered first. "She and I came with my uncle. We have our tickets if you need to see them."

"I guess that won't be necessary," the man said. "You two look too well dressed to be friends with this hooligan. Besides, you're not toting any doughnuts."

He dragged Frank toward the door. Frank was still squirming and tugging, but the man acted like Frank was no more trouble than a kitten would be to a tiger.

"Ow! Why you. . .you. . .!"

The policeman grabbed his shin with one hand. Frank wrenched free and sped out the door, his bag of doughnuts banging against his side.

"Frank must have kicked him," Ted said.

"Good for him," Esther said in a low voice. "I suppose Frank shouldn't be breaking the law, but that policeman didn't have to treat him so rough."

"Do you want to stay and hear Mr. Joplin play some more?"

Esther shook her head. "I don't feel so cheerful anymore."

"Me, either."

When they were walking down the Midway once more, Esther looked at her ruined hat. "Maybe I should throw this away. I could tell Mother I lost it."

"You could," Ted agreed, "but that would be lying."

Esther sighed and nodded.

Ted stopped suddenly. Esther turned around. "What's wrong?" she asked. "You look like you've seen a ghost."

"I was having so much fun seeing the Midway with Frank that I forgot all about the time. Do you think Richard and

Anna are still waiting for us?"

She groaned. "Oh, no! We'd better hurry."

They sped up the street. Esther tried to watch where she was going. She didn't want to run anyone else down!

Richard and Anna were nowhere to be seen near the entrance to Old Vienna, where they'd agreed to meet.

Esther's heart dropped to her shoes. This day was going from bad to worse.

"Come on." Ted's voice sounded grim. "We'd better see if we can find your parents. Maybe they're still at the restaurant."

Neither spoke as they rushed along. Esther wondered whether Ted was as nervous as she was about seeing her parents.

"They *are* waiting for us here," Esther said, relieved when the restaurant came in sight.

Her mother and Anna were seated on a bench outside the restaurant. Richard was standing beside the bench with his arms crossed and an impatient look on his face. Her father was pacing, hands in his pockets.

Esther and Ted glanced at each other, took deep breaths, and hurried across the street. "Hello!"

"There you are!" Esther's father glared at them. "We've been worried sick about you and had no idea where to look in the miles of fairgrounds."

Esther and Ted stood quietly while the four older people scolded them for being late and not staying with Richard and Anna. They knew better than to try to make excuses for themselves.

"We're sorry," Esther said when there was a break in the scolding. "We know we were wrong to be so late."

"Everything was so exciting to see," Ted added. "We were having so much fun that we forgot we were to meet Richard and Anna."

"We forgot all about time." Esther swung her arms wide.

Her mother stared at Esther's hand. "Whatever did you do to your new sailor hat?"

Esther gulped. She'd been hiding the hat behind her skirt when they came up to her parents. In explaining about the time, she'd forgotten she was holding it. "It, uh, it kind of got crushed."

"That is obvious," her mother said dryly. "How?"

Esther glanced at Ted. She didn't much like the pity she thought she saw in his almost-black eyes. "It, um, fell on the ground, and someone crushed it."

"How could it fall on the ground? Weren't you wearing hat pins to secure it to your hair?"

"Well, yes."

"Tell me the *whole* story, Esther Marie."

How does she always know when I'm not telling the complete truth? Esther wondered as she started the story of knocking over the wheeled chair.

"Was the woman hurt?" her father asked.

"No," Esther answered.

Mother shook her head. "When are you going to learn to act like a young lady?"

Esther bit her lip. *Why can't I just act like me?* she wanted to ask. She'd been told often enough that one of a mother's duties was to raise her children to act properly.

Father crossed his arms over his jacket and vest. "Unless you two prove to us that you can act more responsibly, you will not be allowed to visit any exhibits by yourself."

"Yes, sir," Esther muttered.

"Yes, sir," Ted said quietly.

Instead of going back to the hotel, they ate in a German restaurant on the fairgrounds. Bouncy tunes from a German band gave them something to listen to while they ate.

The cheerful music didn't lighten Esther's heart. She

couldn't forget Frank. *It must be awful to be hunted by the fair police just because you're trying to make a living for your family,* she thought.

After dinner the family visited the Minnesota Building while waiting for darkness.

"When darkness falls," Father told them, "the main fair buildings are decorated with light, and there is a fireworks display."

Leaving the Minnesota Building, Esther overheard a well-dressed middle-aged woman say to the woman beside her, "This fair seems a horrid waste of money. There are so many people out of work in the country. The money spent on the fair buildings would be better spent helping them."

The woman beside her agreed.

Guilt settled down on Esther's shoulders like a heavy cape. *Maybe I shouldn't be enjoying this trip to the fair when boys like Frank and Erik have to work,* she thought.

Later that evening, sitting in the dusk in the middle of the White City, Esther admitted the site was beautiful. White lights chased each other along, outlining the buildings, framing them against the night sky. She'd never seen anything like it.

The water in the fountains sprayed up in many colors. "How do they do that?" she asked.

Richard knew, of course. "There are lights beneath the fountains. They shine up from beneath the water and make the water look like it's pink or green or blue."

Soon the fireworks were set off. They were beautiful against the night sky. But as beautiful as everything was, Esther couldn't seem to get excited about it.

Her father sat down beside her and slipped an arm around her shoulders. "Tired?"

She shrugged and leaned her head against her father's shoulder. "Maybe a little."

"Is something the matter?" he asked in a low voice. "You aren't your usual cheerful self."

She bit her bottom lip, wondering how she could tell him what was bothering her. She didn't want to get in trouble for going to exhibits with Frank.

"When I tipped over that wheeled chair this afternoon, I knocked over someone else, too. A boy. He was selling doughnuts."

"Was he hurt?" That always seemed to be her doctor father's first question.

"No," she answered. "But, he was the same age as Ted and me. His father lost his job so he had to quit school and go to work like Erik."

"That's happened to a lot of boys during these hard times," her father said quietly.

"I feel bad, playing and visiting the fair when Frank and Erik have to work."

He squeezed her shoulder. "I'm glad you have such a good heart."

His words made her feel loved, but she still felt guilty.

"Chicago's mayor is trying to help the unemployed men," Father explained. "He's started something he calls an unemployment bureau to help men like Frank's father find jobs."

"Tonight I heard a lady say that instead of spending money on the fair, the country should have given the money to the poor men who are out of work."

"Mmmm." Her father thought about her words for a minute. "I think the fair was good for the unemployed people. How many people do you think have jobs working at this fair?"

Esther looked at him in surprise. "Lots. Too many to count."

"When I see all the wonderful inventions at the fair," her father continued, "they remind me of the incredible things human beings are capable of doing, especially when they work together. One hundred years ago we couldn't have seen the lights that make the buildings so beautiful against the sky tonight."

"They weren't invented one hundred years ago."

"That's right. People wanted better light at night, so people worked and worked until they found a solution. The inventions at the fair give me hope that men will find an answer to our money problems, too. After all, we can see there are a lot of smart people in our world."

Esther looked up at the fireworks bursting in pops and roars against the black sky. Her guilt eased and peace took its place.

Dear God, she prayed silently, *please help the smart people in our country find a way to help Frank and Erik's fathers and the other people who are out of work. In Jesus' name, Amen.*

When they left the fair, they walked along Lake Michigan back to the Beach Hotel. The breeze off the lake felt good. Esther liked the sound of the white-tipped waves that crashed against the boardwalk.

She glanced back over her shoulder. She could still see the lighted buildings of the White City. *The City of Hope,* she reminded herself.

"I wish there was something I could do so children didn't have to be hungry or live hard lives because their parents are out of work," she whispered to Ted.

"Me, too." His voice sounded sad.

But what can we do? she wondered. *We're only twelve.*

CHAPTER 13

The Falling Statue

Ted and the Allertons stayed away from the fair the next day. It was Sunday, so they went to church and then relaxed for the rest of the day.

There had been big arguments between the people who ran the fair and others over whether or not the fair should stay open on Sundays. The editor of the Minneapolis *Tribune* had even written a column about it. He believed there should be no work done on Sundays unless it was necessary.

The fair planners said most people worked Mondays through Saturdays. That left only Sunday for people who lived in and near Chicago to visit the fair.

In spite of the many people against it, the fair stayed open Sundays. Esther's father said the fair had won the battle but lost the war because not many people visited the fair on the Lord's Day.

The next time they visited the fair, they saw an old black man surrounded by people who were trying to speak with him and shake his hand.

"Excuse me." Father stopped a gentleman in the crowd near the Administration Building. "Is that Mr. Frederick Douglass?"

"Yes."

"I'd certainly like to meet him," Father said.

"I should like to, also." Mother's brows puckered. "It isn't polite to introduce yourself to someone, though."

"You didn't let us talk to Mr. Edison," Esther reminded them.

"I think this is different," Father said. "After all, Mr. Edison was in a discussion with two friends. Mr. Douglass appears to be welcoming the public."

"Who is he?" Ted asked. "Why do you want to meet him so badly?"

"Mr. Douglass is the ambassador to Haiti," Mother told him.

"He's done a great deal for black people," Father added. "He's a brave, intelligent, compassionate man."

"He was born a slave," Mother explained. "He taught himself to read and write. Most slaves weren't allowed to read and write. After the war, freed slaves needed someone who could do both well, like Mr. Douglass. Someone who could speak to the public and the lawmakers."

Father nodded. "Since the Civil War, Mr. Douglass had been fighting for the black people. When slavery was made illegal, blacks became free, but they weren't given all the privileges of white citizens. Mr. Douglass fought hard for the Fifteenth Amendment, which made black men citizens and gave them the right to vote."

"Today at the fair is set aside to honor black people," Mother reminded them. "Mr. Douglass will be speaking."

103

Finally Esther's parents decided they would indeed join the crowd that was trying to meet Mr. Douglass. Richard and Anna were given permission to visit a nearby exhibit. Because of the troubles on Saturday, however, Ted and Esther were told to wait for their parents on the steps of a nearby building.

The cousins sat down on the broad steps, plunked their elbows on their knees, and watched the large group of people trying to reach the balding black man with the ring of bright white hair.

"This is going to take a lo-o-ong time," Ted said.

Esther nodded and felt a little guilty. It was her fault they had to sit here. If she hadn't knocked over the wheeled chair, they wouldn't have met Frank. If they hadn't met Frank, they wouldn't have been late meeting Richard and Anna and her parents. If they hadn't been late, they could be off seeing things, like Richard and Anna.

"Hiya!"

Esther and Ted whipped around at Frank's friendly greeting. The boy was just sitting down on a step above and behind them.

Ted laughed. "Back in the fair again. They can't keep you out. You're as slippery as Houdini."

Frank grinned. Esther thought he liked being compared to the young escape artist.

"Did the policeman catch you after you left Mr. Joplin's?" Esther asked.

"Naw. He's too out of shape ta keep up ta me when I'm runnin'."

"Are you selling doughnuts again today?" Ted asked.

"Nope. Candy," Frank answered. "Candy is easier ta hide than doughnuts. It doesn't take up as much room. And it's easy to sell. Say," he looked puzzled, "why are ya sittin' here? Your feet already tired? The day's just startin'!"

Esther smoothed the palms of her hands over the dark blue skirt that covered her knees. "We're waiting for my parents. They're hoping to meet that man."

"Which ones are yer folks?" Frank asked.

She told him and watched him study them a minute.

"Who's that black man?" he asked.

She told him about Mr. Douglass.

"Scott Joplin told me 'bout him." Frank's face shone with interest as he studied the man in the midst of the crowd. "He's almost a hero. He says blacks were freed from slaveholders, but they are still slaves to the white society."

"Mr. Douglass is speaking today because it's been set aside to honor black Americans," Esther said.

Frank snorted. "Honor black Americans, my eye!"

"What do you mean?" Ted asked. "Isn't this the day when there are special talks and events for black people?"

"Sure it is," Frank agreed, "but it's not what the black people wanted. Scott Joplin told me lots of blacks aren't comin' taday, 'cause they're mad at the fair planners."

"Why?" Esther asked. "Why would they be mad because there's a special day for them?"

Frank wrapped his arms around his knees and leaned forward. "They wanted their own exhibition building, see. They wanted ta show the world everythin' black people have done since the Civil War. The fair planners wouldn't let them do that."

"Why?" Ted wondered.

"They told the blacks ta ask their own states ta let them exhibit in the state's buildin's. None of the states let them."

"That doesn't sound fair," Esther said. "The fair planners let women have their own building."

"Yep." Frank nodded. "But that's not all. Mr. Joplin says blacks can't even work at good payin' jobs at the fair. Instead of being construction workers or clerical workers, they can only have low payin' jobs like street sweepers."

Sadness began to fill Esther again. There were so many unfair, hard things in the world that she couldn't do anything about.

"At least the blacks have this special day," Ted said. "They can tell the world what their people have done."

"And what they want for their future," Esther said.

Esther's parents had made it to the great man's side now. She watched her father remove his hat and shake hands with Mr. Douglass, then introduce her mother to the wise old man.

"Guess I'd better be movin' on." Frank slipped his candy-filled bag over his arm.

Esther wondered if he knew that she and Ted were afraid of having her parents find him with them. Did Frank think they were embarrassed of him because he didn't dress or talk as well as they did? She hoped not, but she knew her parents wouldn't approve of their friendship, especially her mother.

Frank stood up. "I'm goin' over ta Wooded Island for a bit. At least there's some shade there. If ya get a chance, come on over and look me up."

The kids watched him walk jauntily down the steps and cross the wide bridge to the island. "I wonder if we'll ever see him again," Ted said.

After lunch, Father and the boys wanted to go to the Horticulture Building. Mother gently argued to visit the Woman's Building instead. Finally it was agreed the men would go to the Horticulture Building and the women to the Woman's Building.

"I want to see the Woman's Building," Esther told her mother as they climbed the steps, "but I'd like to see the Horticulture Building, too."

"So would I," Mother admitted. "However, there isn't time to see everything before we leave. If the men aren't smart enough to want to visit the Woman's Building, we'll have to visit it ourselves."

They enjoyed the model kitchen, but Esther thought the model hospital was more interesting. "I've never even been in a *real* hospital," she told Anna.

The young woman guide in the model hospital told them of the history of women nurses and doctors. "There are almost 250 women doctors in Chicago now," she said proudly.

Anna gasped. "That many? There are women doctors in Minneapolis, too, but I didn't know so many women had become doctors."

The guide smiled. "Isn't it wonderful? Women have entered every area of work that men enter. There are women artists and writers, lawyers and merchants, journalists and editors, cotton planters and teachers, real estate agents and architects, and anything else of which you can think. All the art in this building is by women. A woman even *designed* this building. This is a marvelous time to be a woman!"

"Yes," Mother agreed, "and it will be a better time to be a woman once all women in the country have the right to vote."

Esther looked at her mother in surprise.

"Why, Mother, I didn't know you believed in suffrage for women," Anna said in a voice that sounded as surprised as Esther felt.

Mother looked at them serenely. "Of course I believe women should have the right to vote. We have the benefits of living in America. It is only right that we should have more of the responsibilities."

Anna stared at her. "But you've never gone to any women's suffrage meetings or marched in any of their parades or. . .or anything."

"I shouldn't think a woman needed to carry a poster down the street and holler unseemly things at men to prove to the world she has the intelligence to vote for the people she wants in the government."

Esther and Anna exchanged amused glances as they followed their mother down the hall to the next exhibit area. Esther had never heard her quiet, ladylike mother speak in such a manner. *What else does she think about a woman's place that she hasn't told us,* she wondered.

Esther stood in the middle of the building's Great Hall. She craned her neck to see everything beneath the two-story ceiling.

She stopped beside a small sculpture of a mother sitting beside a cradle with a tiny baby inside. She touched the mother's arm and smiled. *I wish I could make something as beautiful as this,* she thought.

"This is the best part of the whole building!" Esther told Anna as they stared at the seventy-foot murals on the walls.

One of the murals was called "Modern Woman." In it, women were dressed in up-to-date clothing, chased fame, and worked together picking the fruits of knowledge and science.

Esther leaned her head from one side to the other, studying the mural. "Isn't it beautiful, Anna? I wonder how the painter made it so bright."

"It's painted in the modern impressionist style," Anna told her. "Mary Cassatt is the artist."

Esther backed up, trying to get a better view of the huge picture.

Thud!

She came to a sudden halt when she backed into something solid.

"Esther!"

At the sound of Anna's strained voice, Esther whirled around. She'd backed into the base that held the sculpture of the mother and child. The base teetered. Esther and Anna grabbed for it at the same time. The beautiful sculpture slipped from its perch.

CHAPTER 14

One Accident Too Many

Esther's eyes slammed shut. The heavy wooden base thudded against the floor. She held her breath, waiting for the crash of the beautiful sculpture and her mother's "Esther Marie Allerton, how *could* you!"

Neither came.

Instead she heard Anna's voice saying, "Thank you."

Esther opened her eyes. A tall young woman in a navy blue suit was on her knees, the sculpture in her arms. Her face beneath dark hair was almost as white as the marble sculpture.

"You caught it!" Esther clasped her hands together. "I am *so* glad. I thought there was no chance it could be saved, and it is so beautiful!"

The young woman smiled, still hugging the piece to her

chest. "It is lovely, isn't it?"

Mother, who had been viewing a piece at the other end of the hall, hurried up. Her gloved hands lifted her skirt a couple inches above her ankles so she could walk faster. Her pretty face was filled with concern.

Esther bit back a groan and stood up. "I know, Mother, it's my fault. I should have been watching where I was going, but I was looking at the mural."

Her mother's worried glance found the sculpture in the young woman's arms. "It wasn't broken?"

The woman set the piece on the floor beside her and stood up. "No, ma'am."

Mother put a gloved hand over her heart, closed her eyes, and gave a sigh of relief. "Esther Marie, you shall be the death of me yet."

Esther's cheeks burned. It was embarrassing to have her mother speak to her that way in front of the smart-looking young woman who had saved the sculpture.

The woman smiled at her and gave her a quick wink. "The accident could have happened to anyone. Nothing was broken. No harm was done."

A little of Esther's guilt and most of her embarrassment were washed away by the woman's kind words.

"I am Miss Enid Yandell," the rescuer said.

Esther's mother introduced the three of them. Then together, they righted the base. Miss Yandell set the sculpture carefully on top of it. "There! Everything is as good as new."

Esther frowned slightly. "Miss Enid Yandell. We were told that a Miss Yandell made some of the sculptures in the roof garden, but that can't be you. You're too young."

Miss Yandell laughed. "I'm twenty-two, and I did indeed make the garden sculptures. Have you seen them?"

When she found they hadn't been to the cafe in the garden

on the building's roof, she invited them to join her there for coffee. Esther was thrilled when her mother agreed.

It was sunny and breezy on the roof. The garden was lovely. Mother and Anna walked about, enjoying the plants and flowers. But Esther thought Miss Yandell's sculptures were lovelier than the flowers and told her so.

Miss Yandell pointed to some huge sculptures. "See the angels on the edge of the roof? They were sculpted by a girl of nineteen."

"Nineteen!" Esther looked at the huge winged sculptures in wonder. "How did you and this girl get to be so good so young?"

Miss Yandell smiled. "Remember the fair's motto?"

"Yes. It's 'I will.' "

"That's right. If you are willing to work hard for the things you want, you will be surprised at the doors that open for you."

Esther was glad for the oriental awnings that covered the cafe and shaded them from the bright sun when they sat down for coffee and desserts.

A group of well-dressed women stopped at their table to say hello to Miss Yandell. When the sculptress introduced the women to her, she was glad she'd worn one of Anna's hats today. Every one of the women was famous: Jane Adams, Susan B. Anthony, Frances Willard, and Anna Julia Cooper.

Jane Adams was known for her concern for the working people. "She's speaking at the World Labor Congress about the poor working conditions of women and children," Miss Yandell told them.

Frances Willard was known all over the country for her work with the Women's Christian Temperance Union, which tried to make the sale of liquor illegal.

Anna Julia Cooper was a black woman. She had an important position with the Colored Women's League. She spoke often to important groups, telling them that no one should be given or denied special favors because of their gender or race.

Susan B. Anthony impressed Esther the most. She was one of the main leaders of the women's suffrage movement. People either thought she was wonderful or awful.

Mother nodded politely to each women as she and the girls were introduced to them. She spoke a sentence or two to each, thanking them for the work they were doing.

Esther turned to Mother. "Why are you only a mother and housewife, when women can do so many things today?"

She was immediately sorry. She hadn't meant to embarrass her mother. She was relieved when her mother smiled. "Trying to keep you out of trouble keeps me far too busy to work outside the home, Esther."

The adults and Anna laughed. Esther managed a small smile.

A few minutes later, the women left Miss Yandell and the Allertons. Watching them depart, Mother said, "I'm a little surprised to see Anna Cooper here. I heard many blacks were angry because they don't have their own exhibit."

"It's true," Miss Yandell agreed, "that they weren't allowed to set up an exhibit that shows what contributions the black people have made to American history, and that's unfortunate. However, the work of black women artists is displayed in this building."

"Good," Mother said quietly.

Esther thought it was good, too.

"I am glad you believe women have a right to explore their interests, Mrs. Allerton," Miss Yandell said, "even when that means they cannot spend all their time at home." She took a sip of coffee from the delicate china cup. "Let me tell you a funny story.

"Mrs. Ulysses Grant, the widow of the former president and general, visited my sculpting studio one day. At first, I was flattered. Then she told me that a woman's place is in the home.

" 'So you don't approve of me?' I asked.

"Mrs. Grant scowled and said, 'Will you be a better house-wife by your cutting marble?'

" 'Yes,' I answered. 'I am developing muscles in my arms to beat biscuit when I keep house.' "

Mother and the girls laughed. Then Mother asked, "Did she change her mind, then, and decide she approved of your work after all?"

"She did not totally approve, but she felt my work had *some* good purpose."

Esther was sorry when the lovely coffee party was over and they had to leave their new friend to meet Father and the boys.

Her spirits lifted when her father said they were going for a gondola ride before dinner. Clapping her hands, she said, "Oh, I've wanted to ride in one ever since we came to the fair!"

They bought tickets for the gondola. Then they waited in front of the Agricultural Building on wide steps that led to the wooden boat landing at the water's edge, where it would be easier to board the long, narrow boat. On either side of the steps, statues of huge white bulls stared out over the water.

While they waited, Esther told her father and the boys about their afternoon.

"That's nothing." Ted dismissed her afternoon with a wave of his hand. "You should have been with us. We went in a cave! Not a real cave, of course. It was only a model of Mammoth Cave in South Dakota. But it was just like being in a real cave, with stalactites and stalagmites and everything!"

Esther had to admit she would have liked to see that. "But only if I could have my afternoon, too."

A gondola glided silently up to the steps, and Esther and Ted promptly forgot their exciting afternoon experiences.

"Oh, it's one of the prettiest gondolas," Esther cried in delight.

The bow of the gondola was shaped like the head, neck, and back of a swan, with wings raised as if it were about to leave the water. The back of the gondola was the swan's tail. Both the back and front rose taller than a man.

Richard sat on a narrow seat as close to the front of the gondola as he could get. Father took the seat in the back. Anna and Ted shared a seat, and Esther and her mother sat together near the middle of the low-sided wooden boat.

The oarsmen's outfits were brightly colored. Striped shirts matched wide, striped trousers. Colored vests covered the shirts and matched the men's hats. Even brighter sashes were tied about their waists.

The oarsmen—one in front and one in back—made the gondola move across the lagoon as smoothly and quietly as a real swan. They stood while they rowed. The oars were skinny and almost as long as the boat. Another oarsman stood high against the "swan's" tail, controlling the rudder.

The gondola went under a bridge, and they passed from the Great Basin to the lagoon. Ted pointed out white water birds that bobbed along the shore of Wooded Island. Other gondolas, canoes, and canopy-covered electric launches joined them on the water.

As they passed a statue of a warrior with his weapons, Ted asked Esther, "Remember that song we learned? The one about the axe?"

Esther grinned and nodded. Frank had taught them the song. He said all the children in Chicago were singing it.

Ted sang the first line. Then Esther joined in:

Lizzie Borden took an axe
and gave her mother forty whacks.

114

When she saw what she had done,
She gave her father forty one.

They burst into giggles. Richard chuckled.

"Esther Marie!"

Esther looked in surprise at her mother, seated beside her. What had she done now?

"How could you sing such an awful song, let alone laugh at it? I'm ashamed of you. And you, too, Theodore."

Esther spread her hands. "But it's funny!"

Her mother's lips tightened into a thin line. "It most certainly is not funny to sing about a girl killing her parents! The Bible tells us to honor our parents."

"I must agree with your mother," Father said in his severest tone. "Don't let us hear either of you singing that tune again."

Esther and Ted exchanged disgusted looks.

The gondolier who was manning the rudder suddenly broke into song. His beautiful voice rolled out over the water. The music was pretty, but Esther couldn't understand the words. She knew it wasn't the song about Lizzie Borden, though!

"What is he singing?" she asked her mother.

"It's from the opera *Faust*. It's in Italian."

As the gondolier finished his song, Esther saw her new friend walking across a bridge they were approaching.

"There's Miss Yandell, Ted. She's the woman I told you about." She lifted one arm as high as she could. "Miss Yandell! Miss Yandell!"

The woman didn't stop walking or look their way.

"Esther, do stop yelling."

Esther barely heard her mother. She jumped to her feet, waving both arms over her head. "Miss Yandell! Hello, Miss Yandell!"

The gondola started to rock. Esther waved her arms, trying to get her balance. She saw Ted stretch his arms toward her, but he was too far away to reach her. Everyone in her family was yelling at her to sit down. The oarsmen were yelling something in another language.

Her arms waved more wildly. "Help!"

Mother tried to steady her but couldn't. Finally she jumped up and grabbed for Esther.

Too late. *Splash!* Esther held her breath as she hit the water.

CHAPTER 15
Fire!

Esther pushed herself to the surface, sputtering. Her hair clung like wet seaweed to her face. She brushed it out of her eyes with one hand and treaded water with the other.

"Grab the oar, Esther!"

At Ted's order, she looked around for the oar. One of the oarsmen was holding it out to her. She grabbed it and hung on for dear life. She didn't know how to swim, but she knew enough to kick her feet and keep her head above water.

"Help!" *Cough! Cough!* "Help!"

Esther whipped her head around to see who was calling so weakly. "Mother!"

Her mother was trying to wave her arms in the air instead

of moving them in the water. Esther realized in a flash that her mother must have fallen in trying to keep her from falling. Her mother's head slipped beneath the water. Dread swept through Esther. Her mother didn't know how to swim, either!

A moment later, Mother's head popped back up. "Kick, Mother!" Esther called.

Out of the corner of her eye, Esther saw a large dark shape flash by. *Splash!*

Relief swamped her when she saw that it was Father. He was helping Mother.

With Richard and Ted's help, Esther tried to climb into the gondola. It wasn't easy with her high-buttoned shoes full of water and her dress and petticoat soaking wet. She hadn't realized how heavy clothes were when they were wet!

The gondola rocked dangerously when Richard and Ted started to pull her into it. For a minute Esther thought it was going to tip over. Anna and the gondoliers moved their weight to the other side of the boat. A moment later Esther was safe on the bottom of the gondola.

"Thanks." She was panting so hard that she could hardly speak. She brushed her hair off her face again and looked to see if her parents were near the boat yet.

"Why, they aren't even coming to the boat!" she cried.

"I think when Father saw the trouble we were having getting you in the boat, he decided it would be easier to take her to shore," Richard said.

Father had one hand under Mother's chin. She was lying on her back, and he was pulling her along. Richard was right. In a couple minutes, their father reached a small landing and helped Mother up on the steps.

The gondoliers steered for the landing and reached it right after Mother and Father.

Ted and Richard helped Esther out of the gondola. She didn't want their help, but she couldn't manage by herself in the heavy wet dress. Her shoes made squishing sounds when she stepped out onto the paved step.

Fairgoers had seen the accident and surged to the landing to see if Esther and her mother were all right. *There must be hundreds of them,* Esther thought in despair. She turned her back and sank down on one of the bottom steps.

She glanced over at Mother, who was coughing. "Will she be all right?" Esther asked Father.

He nodded, a grim expression on his usually friendly face. "She just swallowed a lot of the lagoon."

Mother, who always took such care to look good in public and act like a lady, looked like something the dog had dragged in. She'd lost her hat. Half her hair had come unpinned and hung in a mass of wet dangles down her back. Her pretty white linen-and-lace gown had turned pale brown and was torn besides. She'd been embarrassed in front of hundreds of people.

Esther dropped her head into her hands. "Am I in trouble now!" she whispered.

A gentle hand touched her shoulder. "Are you all right, Esther?"

She looked up into a concerned face. Miss Yandell! She smiled weakly. "I'm fine, thank you."

I could sure use Houdini's trick box about now, she thought. *I'd like to disappear for good.*

Esther wasn't so fortunate. The next morning, seated on the train on the way back to Minneapolis, she looked from one face to another. No one had a friendly glance for her—not even her cousin Ted.

She'd known her parents would be furious with her. When they decided to cut the trip to the fair short, Ted and her brother and sister had turned against Esther, too. She couldn't blame

119

them. She'd ruined their trip. They didn't get to go to Buffalo Bill's Wild West Show, which was right outside the fair.

Of course, her parents had given her yet another lecture with the old familiar chorus: Why can't you act like a young lady, like Anna?

I wish Mother and Father liked me as much as they do Anna, she thought.

Esther tried to curl deeper into the corner of the plush seat. She looked down at the book in her lap, *David Copperfield.* She pretended to read, but she didn't even see the words. The rhythmic clack of the wheels going around seemed to be saying "Stupid girl! Stupid girl!"

You'd think I'd been punished enough for falling into the lagoon, she thought. After all, the new dress she'd loved had lost its beautiful dark green color. The lagoon water had washed it out and left it a streaked, unwearable mess. Her purse was somewhere at the bottom of the lagoon. Worst of all, wonderful Miss Yandell had seen the whole affair!

She glanced across at Ted and Anna, who were seated on the purple upholstered seat across from her. They both glared at her.

Esther drew her legs up under her skirt and pretended to read once more. It was going to be a long ride home!

The day after they got home, Esther was carrying a large crystal plate piled with cookies. She walked carefully down the hall from the kitchen toward the parlor. The house was filled with family. Uncle Enoch and Aunt Tina, and Ted and his parents, and Ted's brother Walter and his Swedish wife, Lena, had all come to welcome the Allertons back and hear about the fair.

It's good to have people around who will smile and talk to me, Esther thought as she neared the open door to the parlor.

"Tomma tunnor skramla mest!" she heard Lena say, and

smiled. Lena always had a Swedish proverb on the tip of her tongue.

"What does that mean?" Richard asked.

"Empty barrels make the most noise," Lena explained as Esther stepped into the room.

Everyone in the room laughed. "That describes Esther to a *T*," Richard said.

Esther stopped short. Pain stabbed her chest. Had they all been laughing at *her?* Had *she* been the empty barrel? Did sweet Lena truly believe that she had no brains?

The laughter in the room died. Esther realized everyone was staring at her. She could tell they knew she'd heard the unkind remarks.

"I'm sorry, Esther," Lena said in her soft, musical voice. "I spoke without thinking."

Tears blurred Esther's sight and made her eyes hot. She kept her eyes open wide to keep the tears from falling. Carefully she handed the crystal plate to Lena. Then she turned and left the room.

She wanted to run, but she wouldn't let herself. They laughed at her when she didn't act like a lady. So she made herself walk slowly into the hall and up the stairs. Only then, behind her closed door, did she let the tears come.

A week later, Ted was finally speaking to her again, though still he wasn't the friendly cousin he'd always been before.

On a Sunday in the middle of August, they went walking together along the Mississippi River after dinner. Near one of the bridges that spanned the wide water, they met Erik, the newsboy, talking with a young man about twenty-five years old.

Erik's grin spread wide with a welcome that warmed Esther's heart. Then she wondered whether he would still be friendly after Ted told him all the clumsy things she'd done at the fair.

"Haven't seen you two around in awhile," Erik said.

"We've been to Chicago," Ted told him, "to the World's Fair." Erik's eyes opened wide. "No kiddin'!"

"Who are your friends, Erik?" the young man with him asked, pushing his bowler hat toward the back of his curly black hair until Esther thought the hat surely must fall off.

Erik introduced them and then said, "And this is Mr. Thomas Beck. He's a teacher at the Newsboys' Sunday School. He's a newspaper reporter for the Minneapolis *Tribune*, too."

Ted shook Mr. Beck's hand. "I've never met a reporter before."

Esther thought Mr. Beck looked like a reporter. He wore a fashionable brown-and-tan-checked suit with a matching vest. A pencil rested behind one ear. A notebook stuck out of one of his suit pockets.

"Mr. Beck is a good friend of mine," Erik said.

"Tell us about your trip to the World's Fair," Mr. Beck encouraged.

They told them about everything: the beautiful buildings in the White City, the Ferris wheel, the marvelous new inventions and new foods, the huge statues that had seemed to be everywhere in the White City, the famous people they'd seen, the copies of Columbus's ships, even the Houdini Brothers and their trick box. But when Ted started telling them about the electric launches and the gondolas, Esther cringed and grew quiet. Now Erik and nice Mr. Beck would find out what a silly thing she'd done. She stared at the tips of her new high-buttoned shoes—her old ones had been ruined in the lagoon—and waited.

Ted described the gondola and gondoliers. "We all went for a ride in one of the gondolas. One of the gondoliers even sang for us!"

He hesitated. Esther looked up, surprised to find him looking at her.

"And then," Ted started again, "and then we went back to the hotel. The gondola ride was the last thing we did at the fair."

Esther gave him a small smile. He shrugged, lifting the shoulders of his Sunday suit, but he didn't smile back. Sadness pinched her heart. It was going to take a long time for Ted and her family to completely forgive her.

A passerby bumped her elbow. Mr. Beck looked up with a scowl. "Hey, mister, watch where you're going."

The man paid no attention. He was hurrying toward the bridge. Esther saw with surprise that *everyone* was hurrying in that direction or staring and pointing across the river. She and her friends turned to see what was so interesting.

"Fire!" Mr. Beck exclaimed.

Orange flames shot into the air along the opposite bank, where mostly sawmills and homes were built. The flames raced from building to building like a child at play. It seemed only moments before flame covered the riverbank for as far as Esther could see.

Mr. Beck grabbed his pad and pencil. He started across the bridge in a dash, his checkered coat flying out behind him as he ran through the crowd.

Without a second thought, Esther started after him. She could see from the corner of her eye that Ted and Erik were coming, too. Toward the other end of the bridge, she began to feel the heat of the huge blaze. Policemen were warning people to stay back for fear of their lives.

"I'm a *Tribune* reporter," she heard Mr. Beck tell one of the policemen. "I need to get through so I can report on this."

With a shake of his head and another warning to watch out for his safety, the policeman let him through.

Esther leaned against the bridge railing to get a better look at the burning bank. "Ouch!" She drew back, shaking her hands. "That railing is hot!" she told Ted and Erik.

The clanging of fire engine bells alerted the crowd, and the people pressed together to let the firemen by. The roar of the fire drowned out the rattle of the wheels carrying the engines and the hooves of the horses pulling them. The horses were covered with foam, already overheated from pulling the engines as fast as they could. Firemen hanging onto the fire wagons were covered to their chins in rubber coats. Sponges that would protect their mouths hung about their necks.

Wagons of every description began crossing the bridge from the burning side of the city, pulled by terrified horses. Household furnishings and frightened people filled the wagons. Men, women, and children clung to the wagons' sides. Their eyes were huge with fear.

At the sight of them, Esther's excitement died. She only wished she could do something to help them.

Clouds of gray and black smoke and columns of orange and red flames rose so high they almost met the sky. Esther and the boys watched small boats filled with more people move out of the smoke-covered bank.

"There's goin' to be a lot more people without jobs now," she heard Erik say, "and without homes, too."

CHAPTER 16
Esther's Prayer

Erik was right, Esther thought a few days later when she, Ted, Erik, and Mr. Beck again stood beside the river and looked across at the smoldering ashes that had once been over a mile of buildings. Even the part of the bridge they'd stood upon Sunday had been burned. Many sawmills had been completely destroyed. Over 160 houses had been burned, leaving more than 200 families homeless.

"I can't imagine losing my home and everything I own," Ted said, shaking his head.

"At least the people have places to stay," Mr. Beck told them. "A church and two large halls have been opened for them.

People and businesses have donated food, clothing, beds, and blankets."

"It must be awful to live that way," Esther said.

"It's not the same as having a home," Mr. Beck admitted, "but at least they won't have to live under the stars until the men find jobs and can afford to move their families into houses."

"The city is helping the men to find jobs, too." Erik's voice sounded bitter. "The city is even giving work to the men in return for their family's food and shelter."

Esther frowned. "Why does that make you so mad, Erik? It sounds like a good thing."

"Why should the city make jobs for these men when they don't make jobs for men like my pa? He and thousands like him can't help being out of work anymore than these people."

The anger and pain in Erik's eyes sliced through Esther's heart.

August slipped into September. Ted and Esther went back to school, where they spoke to their classes and wrote essays about their trip to the World's Fair.

Oklahoma Territory opened former Cherokee land to settlers. On September 16, one hundred thousand people raced over the land to claim their own acres.

"The paper says a lot of the people are unemployed and came from other parts of the country," Esther told Ted. "I wonder if any of them are from Minneapolis."

Ted shrugged his shoulders. "Maybe, but we know Erik's father isn't one of them."

"Maybe Frank's father is," she said. Of course, they'd never know. It wasn't likely they'd ever again see the tough boy they'd met at the World's Fair.

Sadness slipped over her when she thought of Frank and Erik. She wished for the hundredth time that she could do something to help children whose fathers were out of work. She remembered the White City and her father's words about hope. Looking out the window at the gray, rainy fall day, she whispered, "It's hard to have hope sometimes."

Mayor Eustis opened an unemployment bureau, like the Chicago mayor had done. Walter told Ted and Esther that the labor unions were pleased about that. Was the unemployment bureau a sliver of hope? Esther wondered.

One day after school when she and Ted went to meet Erik and Mr. Beck, she brought a copy of the Minneapolis *Tribune* with her.

She opened it noisily to the article she wanted and pointed it out to Mr. Beck.

"Look at this! It says, 'The army of the unemployed is on the decrease. Nearly all who want work have found it.' " She glared at the reporter. "How can the newspaper print lies like that?"

Mr. Beck shoved his bowler toward the back of his black curls and spread his hands. "What makes you think it's a lie?"

Erik snorted. "Most anyone would know it. I know lots of men who need jobs."

Ted nodded. "My brother Walter says the labor unions are helping out a lot of their members' families."

"Walter's wife, Lena, is Swedish," Esther said. "The Scandinavians are trying to help their own people, like the labor unions are doing. Lena says there are many Swedish men here out of work. Many of the men send money back to relatives in Sweden. Now they can't send money back because they haven't got jobs. They can't even pay for their own food and rent."

Mr. Beck nibbled on the end of his pencil. "It's true there're very few people coming to America from other countries now. Since the panic began, for the first time in our country's history,

127

more people are leaving the nation than entering it."

"You see?" Erik challenged. "Everyone but the city leaders knows how bad things are."

"If you want to be a newspaperman one day, Erik, you have to learn to deal with facts," Mr. Beck said. "The truth is, no one knows how many people are unemployed in the city. No one has counted the unemployed."

Erik lifted his chin and glared at Mr. Beck. "You always say newspapers make people aware of important things in the world. Why don't you write an article saying the city needs to count the unemployed men?"

Mr. Beck stared at Erik for a moment. "Maybe I'll do that." He pushed himself up from the wooden bench outside the soda fountain where they'd met. "I'd better get to work."

Esther crossed her arms and watched him walk down the street. The adults in the city weren't doing nearly enough about the jobless. It was so frustrating!

"I'm going to find a way to help jobless people," she declared in a low voice.

Erik and Ted whooped with laughter.

"You're only twelve!" Erik reminded her.

"What makes you think you can do more than adults?" Ted asked.

Her cheeks burned from their laughter. For a moment she was tempted to take her words back. Then she remembered the women artists at the World's Fair.

"Remember the motto of the World's Fair?" she asked the boys. "I will."

Erik chuckled. "A couple little words aren't goin' to help people get jobs and food and rent."

A trickle of doubt slid into her mind. She pushed it away. "The Bible says, 'I can do all things through Christ, who strengthens me.' If we ask God to show us something to do to help people, I'm sure He will. Will you two pray with me?"

Ted looked like he wasn't sure God would really answer them, but he agreed.

Erik just shook his head. "I think you're bein' foolish. God hasn't helped my family in all these months. Why should He help now?"

"You're wrong about God not helping your family," Esther said quietly. "He gave you a job as a newsboy to help your family, didn't He? I wish He would have given your father a job instead, but things would be worse if you didn't have a job, either."

Erik kicked at a brown leaf. "I still say you're foolish."

"I don't care." Esther lifted her chin. "I'm going to ask Him to show us a way to help anyway."

CHAPTER 17
The Plan

The logs in the parlor fireplace crackled and gave off a warm glow. Outside a late November snowstorm howled, whistling around corners and sending an occasional puff of wind down the chimney.

It's cozy here, Esther thought. She poked a needle through the gray wool school dress she was mending and glanced around the parlor.

Ted's mother and his sister-in-law, Lena, were spending the evening with Esther, Anna, and Mother. The women at church had collected used clothing. It had been sent home with the women to mend before being given to the poor.

"Isn't this lovely?" Lena held up a long black wool cape with a high collar trimmed in black velvet. "It barely needs any repair."

Mother smiled. "I'm glad so many people are giving things that haven't been worn to shreds. Every mother wants to be able to dress her family well."

"Have you girls bought your Christmas dresses yet?" Aunt Alison asked Esther and Anna.

Esther glanced at Anna and bit her bottom lip. "We. . .we don't need new dresses this year," she finally answered.

Aunt Alison raised her eyebrows in surprise. Her hand stopped with the needle above the brown trousers she was mending. "But both of you love pretty clothes!"

Anna bent over the child's red knit bonnet she was working on. "We decided to remake our dresses from last year instead."

"Oh." Aunt Alison and Lena gave the two girls funny looks but didn't ask any more questions.

Esther breathed a small sigh of relief. She was glad Anna hadn't said more. It would have sounded so proud. Last Sunday the pastor had spoken on giving to the poor. "If you find ways to save money," he'd said, "you will have money to give to those who need it more." She and Anna had decided to give away the money they saved by not buying new Christmas outfits. Their parents had agreed they could do so.

But I don't think that's the answer to my prayer, Esther thought.

She didn't think helping the church women was the answer either, though she was glad to mend and sort clothes with them. *There must be something special God has that children can do together to help,* she thought.

At least Mr. Beck had written an article suggesting the city count the number of people without jobs. So far, the city hadn't done anything about it.

"It's going to be cold walking to school tomorrow." Anna pretended to shiver.

"Can we put a pot of oatmeal on the back of the stove

tonight, so it will be ready to eat for breakfast?" Esther asked her mother. It always seemed easier to face a winter morning with warm oatmeal in her stomach.

She wondered how many of the jobless men's families would have warm breakfasts.

"Oh!"

Mother leaned forward. "Did you poke yourself with the needle?"

Esther shook her head. "No, I'm fine." She knew now what she wanted to do to help.

Esther searched out Ted first thing the next morning at school and told him her plan.

"I think that's a great idea," Ted said. "Let's ask Mr. Timms right away if we can do it."

Mr. Timms listened carefully, then nodded so fast that his round cheeks bounced. "Wonderful! We've a few minutes before school starts. Let's go speak to the superintendent about your plan right away."

A nervous lump formed in Esther's throat as the three of them hurried toward the superintendent's office. She'd never actually talked to the head of the entire school before.

When they entered his office, the superintendent lifted his bald head. "What can I do for you?"

"The children have a wonderful plan, sir. I thought you should hear of it right away." Mr. Timms put a hand on Esther's back and urged her forward.

She gulped and wiped her sweaty palms down the sides of her dress. "My cousin Ted and I, we wanted to help the families of some of the jobless men. So we thought. . .that is. . ." She swallowed again.

"Go on," Mr. Timms urged.

"Could the students bring food to the school to give to

132

their families?" The question came out in a rush. "I mean, if every student in the school brought just one thing, we'd have a lot of food to give."

The superintendent folded his hands on his desk and thought a moment. "Where would you collect the food?"

"We could put baskets in each classroom," Esther suggested.

"And how would you get the food to the jobless men's families?" the superintendent asked.

"I thought we could give it to the city's Associated Charities," she answered. "We could ask some of the students whose fathers' businesses have wagons to take the food we collect to the charities offices."

A thin smile spread across the man's face. "It seems you've thought of everything. Very well, Mr. Timms. Please arrange for these two to speak in all the classrooms this afternoon. Now you'd best all get to your class. The morning bell will be rung any minute now."

A couple days each week, Esther and Ted had fallen into the habit of going home from school by way of a street on which Erik often sold newspapers. Today when they saw him, Mr. Beck was with him.

"We have something so exciting to tell you!" Esther told Erik almost before she finished saying hello.

Mr. Beck laughed. "If this is important, why don't we go inside the soda fountain across the street? I'll treat you all to hot cocoa while you tell us your news."

"What do you think?" Esther asked eagerly when she'd told them her plan.

Erik and Mr. Beck both thought the plan was great. "But you should get more of the schools involved," Erik said, lifting his mug of fragrant warm cocoa.

"Someone should write a short article about the plan," Mr.

Beck suggested. "The article could be distributed to the schools. Why don't you do that, Erik?"

Erik almost spit out the cocoa he'd just sipped. "Me?"

Mr. Beck nodded. "You want to be a writer, don't you?"

"But. . .but that's just a dream."

"If you write the article, I'll check it over and correct the mistakes," Mr. Beck assured him. "That is, if you make any mistakes. I'll ask the *Tribune* editor if he'll have his staff print copies of it."

Erik wrapped his hands around the warm mug. "Do you really think I can write it?"

Mr. Beck pushed his bowler back on his curls. "Wouldn't have suggested it if I didn't. Every writer has to start someplace."

Ted remembered what James Hill had told him and Erik last summer: *Believe in your dreams and a way will open.* Was this a way for Erik's dream to begin to be real? Would he take it or let it pass by?

"I'll try it," Erik said with a sharp nod.

Mr. Beck said Erik's article was well done. The reporter only changed a couple misspelled words. Later Mr. Beck told them, "When I showed it to the editor, he told me to do a follow-up article when the food has been collected and delivered. Why don't you try writing that one, too, Erik?"

Ted thought Erik couldn't look happier if he'd been handed a bag of gold coins.

The project went better than Ted and Esther ever imagined. The Minneapolis students collected enough food to feed 120 families!

Esther held up her best winter dress, looked it up and down, and sighed. "It's no use, Anna. There's nothing that can make this dress look new again for Christmas."

"Of course there is. You simply haven't given it enough thought. You are too impatient, Esther."

Esther laid the dress over the parlor couch. "I know, but I'm trying to change."

She picked up the sewing basket from beside the fireplace. "Maybe I can find something in here to help." She opened the basket and pulled out ribbons, lace, and buttons her mother had saved from different sewing projects over the years. She held up different pieces against the dress. "Nothing seems to work," she complained.

"Let me try." Anna went through the same process with no success.

"This seemed like such a good idea when Pastor Adams said to be thrifty," Esther told her. "Now it seems hard."

"I know! Do you still have that black velvet dress that you outgrew? We could cut it up and use the material to make a high collar and long cuffs. They'd look wonderful against this purple brocade."

Esther jumped up, excited. "Maybe a wide black velvet tie around the waist, too."

Half an hour later they were busy cutting out the pieces from the old dress and talking happily about their Christmas plans when Ted and his brother Walter stopped by.

"Did you hear about the mayor's new plans to help jobless men?" Ted asked.

The girls hadn't.

"The cold weather has brought so many homeless men to the police station to stay at night," Walter told them, "that the mayor decided to go there and talk with them himself. He found out only two had had anything to eat."

Ted grinned. "So he decided to open a soup kitchen for the unemployed and homeless men who stay at the police station at night. The city leaders are planning to hire jobless men to

135

remove snow from sidewalks and streets and help with road repairs."

"Which the labor unions and others have been asking the leaders to do for quite awhile now," Walter added.

"Best of all," Ted said, "Mayor Eustis has ordered a count of the people in the city who are unemployed and in need."

"Do you think he did that because of Mr. Beck's article?" Esther asked.

"Maybe," Walter said, "but I think meeting and talking to the homeless men helped, too."

"The mayor is asking businesses to donate food so every family that hasn't a way to buy food can be given a Christmas basket," Ted told Esther and Anna.

Esther's heart seemed to grow with joy. "What a wonderful Christmas present for the people!"

Anna frowned slightly. "I think it's wonderful, too, but. . . won't the people be embarrassed to take charity from the city?"

"The mayor thought of that," Walter said. "Unemployed men will make the food deliveries to the families. That way, the people getting the baskets won't feel as badly at others seeing them in hard times."

"I know the food baskets won't fix all the problems for the families of the jobless men," Esther told Ted, "but it's a start."

"At least no one will have to go hungry on Christmas," he agreed.

CHAPTER 18

Christmas Eve

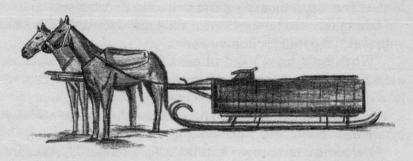

Snow fell in large, fluffy flakes on the afternoon of Christmas Eve. The Allerton house was filled with smells of Christmas baking: sugar cookies and pies in the morning, and now the turkey that was roasting for dinner.

In the parlor, Esther, Anna, and Richard were decorating their Christmas tree with colorful glass ornaments and white strings of popcorn. Ted was helping, just because he liked Christmas trees so much. His family had put their tree up the night before.

The tree stood in the parlor's bay window, where the children could watch the snowfall while they worked. Sleighs and runners on wagons made soft hissing sounds as they passed down the snow-covered streets. The horses' hooves could barely be heard for the snow.

"I like the bells so many people put on the horses this time of year," Esther said. "Their ringing is such a cheerful sound."

A large horse-drawn wagon on runners pulled along the curbstone in front of the Allerton home. "Johnson Brothers Market" was written in large letters on the side of the enclosed wagon. A driver and his partner men sat bundled against the winter weather. Wool blankets kept the horses warm.

The children looked at the wagon curiously. "I didn't think Mother was expecting any more deliveries," Anna said.

One of the men jumped down and jogged toward the house with two flat packages in his hand.

"Why, that's Erik!" Ted hurried toward the front door to meet him with Esther right on his heels. They invited Erik to take off his things and join them in the parlor.

"Can't stay but a minute," he said, standing in the hallway by the front door. "My pa is waiting for me."

"He doesn't have to wait in the cold," Ted said. "Ask him to come inside."

"We have heated stones to keep our feet warm," Erik said, "and lap robes, too. We're delivering Christmas baskets, so we can't stay."

"Did the merchants make a lot of donations?" Esther asked eagerly.

Erik grinned. "The collection point was overflowing with food: flour from flour mills, beef and chicken from meat markets, thousands of pounds of butter from creameries, candy and bread from bakeries, oysters from packing houses, coffee, tea, fish, sugar, and rice from grocers. A town in North Dakota even sent a thousand jackrabbits for the baskets!"

Ted and Esther laughed. "I bet most of the people getting the baskets have never cooked a jackrabbit before," Esther said, "but they'll be glad for them just the same."

Erik sobered. "I heard at the collection point that when the city counted the jobless men, they found there were over eight hundred families who needed help. That's about six thousand people all together."

Ted let out a low whistle. "I knew things were bad, but I didn't know they were that bad."

"And that doesn't include the people who are being helped by unions and other groups," Erik added. "Mayor Eustis and the leaders were really surprised."

A shiver went through Esther, and she rubbed her hands over her arms. How awful to think of so many people without money to buy food!

Ted looked out the oval window in the door. "Why is your father driving Johnson Brothers' wagon?"

"Some of the large merchants donated wagons and teams to deliver the baskets." Erik's eyes were shining. "One of the Johnson brothers was helping put food in baskets and load the wagons. He thought Pa was such a good worker that he's offered him a job. He starts right after Christmas."

Esther bounced up and down in her excitement. "That's wonderful!"

"It doesn't pay nearly as well as the railroad work," Erik said quickly, "but at least he'll have pay comin' in regular."

"That's great," Ted said. "I know the Johnson brothers won't be sorry they hired him."

Erik gave him a grateful smile. "Oh, I almost forgot why I stopped!" He handed each of them a flat package wrapped in brown paper and tied with twine. "Go ahead, open them."

They made quick work of tearing off the paper. Inside were copies of the articles Erik had written about the students' food collection project. The articles were neatly but simply framed.

"They're perfect! Thank you," Esther said. It would be

nice to have something to remember the project that had meant so much to all three of them.

"My pa helped me make the frames for them." Erik shifted from one foot to the other.

"We didn't get anything for you," Esther told him, feeling uncomfortable.

Erik stuffed his gloved hands into his jacket pockets. His cheeks grew redder than they'd been from the cold. "I guess you gave me your present early."

Esther and Ted frowned at him, puzzled.

He cleared his throat. "I mean when you came up with the idea for the students' food collection. I thought you were foolish, but you made it happen. And now my pa has a job, too. I guess you were right. Nothing is impossible with Jesus."

He opened the door and hurried out onto the porch before Esther or Ted could say anything. At the bottom of the steps he turned around and waved. "Merry Christmas!"

That evening after Christmas Eve services, Ted's family and Uncle Enoch and his wife joined the Allertons for Christmas dinner. When Walter had discovered that Thomas Beck hadn't any family in town, he'd invited him to join them, too. Esther and Ted had introduced Walter and Mr. Beck when they were working on the students' food project. Now the two men were fast friends.

When dinner was over, they all visited in the parlor, where the tree ornaments sparkled in the light of the glass-shaded parlor lamps. The children sat on the floor by the tree so there would be enough seats for the adults. The smells of pine, burning logs, and cinnamon from mugs of cider filled the room.

"I must say, your Christmas dresses are lovely," Aunt Alison told Anna and Esther. "If you hadn't told me you were remaking old gowns, I wouldn't have known they weren't new."

Esther and Anna beamed at each other. Aunt Alison's compliment made Esther gladder than ever that they'd decided to follow the pastor's advice and be thrifty.

Uncle Enoch leaned back in his chair and took a sip from his mug of hot cider. "I must say I'm glad 1893 is almost over. I believe it's been one of the hardest years for the country moneywise in this century."

It seemed to Esther that Uncle Enoch, being a banker, always thought of everything in terms of money.

"Banks closing all over the country, people out of work, railroads going bankrupt." Uncle Enoch shook his head. "Yes, indeed, it's been a rough year."

"I'm glad the Great Northern Railroad didn't go bankrupt," Ted said. "For a long time, I was afraid it would. Then Father would have been out of work."

"Then *your* family might have received a Christmas basket." Richard gave him a friendly poke in the side with his elbow.

"It's no laughing matter," Ted's father said. "I had the same worries as Ted. But since everything worked out so well, I rather wish Alison and I had joined Ted and the Allertons at the World's Fair last summer!"

Father chuckled. "It was the experience of a lifetime," he admitted.

"Well, Congress has repealed the Sherman Silver Act," Uncle Enoch said. "That should get the country back in good shape, though it may take awhile."

Esther had no idea what the Sherman Act was, only that it had something to do with silver and paper money. Adults had argued about it a lot during the year. Still, she hoped Uncle Enoch was right about things getting better.

Walter leaned forward, his large hands wrapped around his mug of cider. "Even though this has been a hard year, it's a great time to be alive."

Ted nodded. "Uncle Daniel said something like that when we were at the World's Fair, because of all the wonderful inventions we saw."

"The machines people have made *are* wonderful," Walter agreed, "but I was thinking of a different kind of discovery. There seems to be a new spirit in the land today. People are becoming their brothers' keepers as never before."

"Because of the Christmas baskets?" Esther asked.

"Yes, partly. The city's usually let churches and charities take care of the poor. Now Minneapolis arranged to collect and deliver the Christmas baskets and fuel, too. Chicago, Minneapolis, and other cities have started unemployment bureaus to help jobless men find work. But there are new laws, too, to protect people."

"Like the railroad laws that make trains safer for passengers and brakemen like Erik's father?" Ted asked.

Walter nodded.

"There's another law that goes into effect January first," Mr. Beck reminded them. "Employers will only be allowed to let children under sixteen work between seven in the morning and six in the evening. No more sweatshops where children work themselves into early graves."

Esther remembered Frank and Erik and how hard they worked. She told Mr. Beck about Erik's gift and his father's new job.

Mr. Beck grinned. "It isn't only his father that has a new job. I told my editor that Erik had written those articles about the students' food project and that Erik hopes to be a reporter one day. I haven't had a chance to tell Erik yet, but my editor said Erik can have a job as errand boy at the newspaper if he wants."

"Hurrah!" Ted shouted.

Mr. Beck held up a hand. "He won't be writing any articles,

but at least he can have a chance to be around the business and see if that's what he really wants to do. It pays better than being a newsboy, and he won't have to work out in the rain and snow anymore."

Ted and Esther exchanged grins.

"You two were some of the first in the city to help the unemployed men and their families," Mr. Beck reminded them. "I think your food collection project showed the city's leaders that the need in the city was greater than they thought. Maybe you started some of them thinking about other ways the city could help."

"That's right," Father said. "Our families are proud of both of you."

A few minutes later Esther and her mother went into the kitchen. Together they piled crystal plates with Christmas cookies.

"Your father is right," Mother told her when they were done. "We're very proud of the young woman you've become this year. I used to worry over your impulsive nature. It was always getting you into trouble!"

Esther's spirits sank. Not another lecture! Not on Christmas Eve!

Mother folded her hands at the waist of her elegant Christmas gown and smiled. "Then one day I realized that it's that same energy that used to get you into trouble that you put into the students' food collection project. And I think that is a very good thing. I am very blessed to have such a wonderful daughter."

Esther carefully carried the delicate, cookie-covered plate up the hallway. Lena was playing the parlor piano, and everyone was singing Christmas hymns. But it was her mother's words that Esther was hearing in her heart.

There's More!

The American Adventure continues with *A Better Bicycle*. A new style of bicycle is growing in popularity, and eleven-year-old Peter Morgan is willing to work all summer to buy the royal blue model that has captured his attention. But Peter's attention is also taken by the new family in his well-to-do Minneapolis neighborhood. Peter and his sister Carol notice that the Dawes family has old furniture and wears country clothes.

Now Mattie Dawes misses school because she fell down some steps, but her mother won't let Carol and her friends visit. Then Peter discovers Harry Dawes hiding in the boys' clubhouse in the middle of the night. What is going on? Is there a problem? What can Peter and Carol do to help?